THE THOREAU WHISPERER

Channeling the Spirit of Henry David Thoreau

A True Story

By

Cathryn McIntyre

THE THOREAU WHISPERER

Cathryn McIntyre

Presented by
The Concord Writer
P.O. Box 282
Concord, MA 01742
www.theconcordwriter.com

Published by:

BookBaby
7905 N Crescent Blvd
Pennsauken, NJ 08110

ISBN#: 978-0-9998495-0-7 (softcover)

Library of Congress Number: 2018901058

Printed in the United States of America

Cover Photo by Cathryn McIntyre
Walden Pond, Concord, Massachusetts

Author's Note

The original title of this book was *Thoreau's Wise Silence*, and it has been referred to and quoted from on The Concord Writer website under that title for many years. The title, *Thoreau's Wise Silence* was inspired by this quote from Ralph Waldo Emerson's, *The Over-Soul (1841)*:

> *"We live in succession, in division, in parts, in particles. Meantime within man is the soul of the whole; the wise silence; the universal beauty, to which every part and particle is equally related; the eternal ONE."*

Although the underlying theme continues to be the wise silence, I have chosen to publish this book with the more playful title, *The Thoreau Whisperer*, thus taking advantage of what has become a common expression in our time.

I first heard the term "whisperer" when it was used in Robert Redford's movie, *The Horse Whisperer*, about a man with a special gift for communicating with horses. It was later used in the title of one of my favorite ever television programs, *The Ghost Whisperer*, to describe a woman who has the ability to see and communicate with ghosts.

For this book, I have chosen the title *The Thoreau Whisperer*, to describe a woman who has a gift for communicating with those in spirit and who had the extraordinary opportunity to connect with the spirit of one of America's most treasured writers. That woman is me.

The Thoreau Whisperer is the true story of my experience channeling the spirit of Henry David Thoreau.

- Cathryn McIntyre
February 2018

For All Who Seek The Truth
In Spirit

"Never the spirit was born, the spirit shall cease to be never.
Never was time it was not, end and beginning are dreams."
Bhagavad Gita

THE THOREAU WHISPERER

Channeling the Spirit of Henry David Thoreau

A TRUE STORY

BY

CATHRYN MCINTYRE

INTRODUCTION

Perhaps more than in any other town in America, there is the presence of spirit in Concord, Massachusetts. Because of a place called Walden Pond and because of the activities of one man who was born in Concord 200 years ago, those of us who go there today are reminded of the presence of spirit in our lives. At Walden Pond, we reflect on the messages brought forth in the book he called, *Walden: Or Life in the Woods* (1854), and in many of his other writings. Walden Pond is the place of the silent walk. It is the place where those of us who go there as pilgrims reflect on his observations and on our own spirituality. We walk in silent reverence to man and to God and we contemplate who we are and how we fit into the greater scheme of things. In the words of Henry David Thoreau we find an answer to that question.

While he lived in his cabin at Walden Pond from July 4, 1845 to September 6, 1847, Thoreau observed the change that was taking place between the slower pace of life as it had always been and the newer, faster way of life that was ushered in by the industrial revolution. He wrote about the train that traveled past the pond, describing it as an "iron horse" that disrupted the peace of nature, while enhancing commerce and energizing the people of the town. Life moved faster because the train made it possible to travel into the city more often and for those in the city to travel there, and the faster we can travel, the more experiences we can have, and the more efficiently we work, the more work we can do, and work and attainment become more important than silent reflection, and what is lost is the wisdom about life that comes from taking such an inward journey.

From his post at Walden Pond, Thoreau saw and understood the direction the country and the people were going in and the principles he outlined in *Walden* can still be applied today. In the *Bible* in *Mark 8:36* it is asked, *"For what shall it profit a man, if he shall gain the whole world, and lose his own soul?"* That is the question that Thoreau challenged us to consider and he asked it in many different ways. The silent walker who goes to Walden today goes there seeking the answer to that question as he attempts to connect to the deepest, wisest, most worthwhile part of himself and he feels confident he can do that at Walden.

There is a special energy that is resident at Walden Pond that many who go to the pond can feel. To me it is unquestionably there and I believe it was there in Thoreau's day as well. In my book, *Honor in Concord: Seeking Spirit in Literary Concord* (2008), Alex, who symbolizes a young Thoreau in the fictional story, asks his grandfather whether it was Thoreau who made the pond unique or whether he was simply the first to recognize it as so. His grandfather, Sam, who represents Ralph Waldo Emerson in the story, replies that it was the natural subtle beauty and gentle energy of the pond that had drawn Thoreau there, and that would always draw people there. I believe that to be true.

Contrary to the myth, Thoreau did not live as a hermit at Walden Pond. He states at the beginning of *Walden* that he is one mile from his nearest neighbor. In fact it was a short one mile walk into the village from the pond and thus to his family home, where he would have found company and meals to supplement those he was able to stir up for himself at the pond, and Walden Pond itself was not a hermitage. In *Walden,* Thoreau talks about the many industries operating at the pond, from the ice makers in winter, to the hunters and fisherman. Still, Thoreau was devoted to the goals he set out for himself when he moved there, to live deliberately and with self-sufficiency and economy, to prove that man could live with less and yet have a deeper experience of life. He made daily excursions into nature and carefully recorded his observations in the journals that he kept while living there, journals that he later transformed into his book, *Walden.* At Walden Pond, Thoreau learned to connect to that place of calm within himself, the place that Emerson called *the wise silence.*

* * *

For years I have debated with fellow writers, readers and teachers of mine over the issue of whether it is necessary to know the details of a writer's life in order to better understand his or her work. On one side of the debate are those like myself who feel it is impossible to understand the work of any individual without also understanding the events of the life that formed their point-of-view and on the other side are those who believe that it is the quality of the idea that matters, and not the messenger of the idea. Early on in the process of communication that led to the creation of this book I received the following:

> If a man passes you on the street, asks for the time and then distills upon you a few words at the right moment that change your life, it doesn't matter who that messenger might be. It doesn't matter whether he comes from the farm on the nearby hill or from the ghetto in the city that is two hundred miles south. It doesn't matter what his circumstances or his character. It is the idea that is most important, not the messenger.

> So we stand and watch as the man continues his walk down the street, and we think and rethink his message to us. The message may be universal or simple, it may be something that reminds us of something that was once said to us at another time in just that way, and in that moment we recognize that spirit is at work in our lives, and we pause and reflect, and maybe we then look at life in another way.

Again, it seems it is the message not the messenger that is most important, still, I find my experience of any written work richer when I am well informed as to the history of the man or woman behind the work. Might I be persuaded by the ideas regardless of the writer's background, possibly, but will I more fully identify with the writer, and more fully grasp his or her message if I can understand it through the context of the story of their lives? My answer to that is an enthusiastic yes.

So, as I began to organize the materials that I had amassed during an extraordinary episode in my own life that began in November 2006 when I first tapped into the stream of words that later became the substance of this book, I was faced with the question of how I was going to present this material to a world that might not be willing to believe that it was in fact what I believed it to be. Even for readers who knew it was possible for those of us in the physical world to communicate with those who are not those same readers would still want to know why what I have come to refer to as *the enduring spirit of Henry David Thoreau* would be talking to me.

What I concluded was that just like in my book, *Honor in Concord* where I shared stories from my own life juxtaposed with a fictional story in order to portray an even broader view of reality than I was hinting at in that fictional story, in *The Thoreau Whisperer* I would need to share stories from my own life again, this time juxtaposed with the words I had received from Thoreau in order to provide the context in which those words were received. *The Thoreau Whisperer* thus began to take shape around the sharing of particular events in my life that took place leading up to and during January of 2006 and in the years that followed when this phenomenon was taking place. There were many cases when those incidents prompted the discussion of some of the topics that are covered within the materials that are presented in this book.

There are many today who have the courage to speak the truth about their own experiences communicating with those in spirit. Mediums like, John Edward, James Van Praagh and George Anderson, and near death experiencers like Dannion Brinkley and Dr. Eben Alexander are examples of some who I admire that have had the courage to share their experiences, their beliefs and their abilities and to forge a trail for others like myself who have similar gifts to follow. Thoreau is also someone I admire for having had the courage to speak the truth of his own beliefs during his lifetime and, within the pages of *The Thoreau Whisperer,* he does this again as he reminds us of the fundamental truths that have always been there in the words he left behind.

I present this material then as honestly and forthrightly as it was presented to me, and I include information about my own life only when I feel it is needed to provide context; to help to answer the question of why me; or simply to share some of my memories of an experience that was to me sheer magic. The material I believe originates with Thoreau himself is presented as I received it, with some editorial and organizational changes, but I leave it up to you who read this book to decide for yourselves whether the source of the material is in fact the spirit who once lived a life as Henry David Thoreau. Whatever its source, I hope you will recognize the value in the wisdom that this book contains.

The other party in the extraordinary collaboration that led to the creation of this book was my mentor, Thoreau scholar, Bradley

P. Dean, Ph.D. Brad Dean gained international recognition when he edited and published two of Thoreau's unfinished manuscripts, *Faith in a Seed* (1993); *Wild Fruits* (2001), as well as a collection of Thoreau's letters to H.G.O. Blake entitled, *Letters to a Spiritual Seeker* (2004). Brad was at work on a compilation of Thoreau's Indian notebooks when he passed suddenly in January 2006 and it was soon after Brad's passing when this most extraordinary episode in my own life began.

Cathryn McIntyre

TRUTH

"Truth strikes us from behind and in the dark, as well as from before and in broad daylight."

Henry David Thoreau,
Journal, November 5, 1837.

"It is not enough that we are truthful; we must cherish and carry out high purposes to be truthful about."

Henry David Thoreau
Letter to H.G.O. Blake, July 21, 1852

"The day is never so dark, nor the night even, but that the laws at least of light still prevail, and so may make it light in our minds if they are open to the truth."

Henry David Thoreau
Letter to H.G.O. Blake, December 19, 1854

"In the light of a strong feeling, all things take their places, and truth of every kind is seen for such."

Henry David Thoreau
Journal, January 1, 1852

"If I can do no more, let my name stand among those who are willing to bear ridicule and reproach for the truth's sake, and so earn some right to rejoice when the victory is won."

Louisa May Alcott
Letter to American Woman Suffrage Association,
October 1885

THE THOREAU WHISPERER

Chapter One
How It Began

"I am born, David Henry Thoreau, in this American town,
in this place called Concord."

Concord, Massachusetts, July 12, 1817

In the garden of a house on Virginia Road in Concord, Massachusetts, a man stands listening to the cries of his wife indoors. Their third child, a son, is about to be born. This child, second son to this man and his wife, will become one of America's most famous writers and philosophers and his words will be remembered for generations to come. Today he is a babe, crying as he is brought into the world and handed to his mother who holds him close to her. She has not died during childbirth as many other women of her time have done, and she will outlive him and all but one of her four children. His father is soon called in to her side to see his new son, and later his older brother and sister are allowed in to welcome him. His grandmother, whose home they now occupy is also there. This family will form a circle of love and protection around this infant that he will rely on for all of his life and that will continue on after his death.

It is a gentle sun that shines on the house this day to welcome this God-child into the world. He is a child of the nature that surrounds him and a child of spirit, and there is wisdom in the wind that brings his spirit to life. Had he once lived in Judea eighteen hundred years before, as he will later recall? Had the stars looked down on him when he was a shepherd in Assyria in the same way they will look down on him here in New England? If reincarnation is true perhaps so, but who he was before will little matter after this life that will leave the world so much.

His first steps are taken in their home in Chelmsford and it is his Aunt Sarah who teaches him. He walks across the wood floor, teetering before falling, and is quickly swept up and set back on his feet so that he might try it again. These are the same feet that will one day walk every inch of Concord and now they struggle to cross from the kitchen table to the coarse blanket that covers the arm of the rocking chair. He hears sounds in the distance, the birds sing and he pauses and listens for his hearing is clear and his mind is sharp and he is taking it in, even then.

He makes his way to the door often, anxious to go outside and join his brother and sister in the yard as they move about in play. This boy of one clings to the side of the porch step while he smiles and laughs at his brother and sister, and then, distracted by a butterfly, his eyes look away.

Inside the house his father arrives home and drops a satchel onto the table. It is full of the items he has purchased from the general store in town. His mother will make the bread and the pudding that will keep this family alive, while his father struggles to find another means to make a living. He cannot go on living off the kindness of his wife's family or his own, so he has begun to make plans to move his family into Boston. There he will start another business, on King Street[1] near Faneuil Hall. There he will work hard for little profit, but feel some satisfaction as a man who is providing for his growing family. In 1821 the last of his four children will be born, another daughter. There will be two sons and two daughters.

---

[1] Now known as State Street.

This is the beginning of Thoreau's life, this family setting of gentle, kind people, who struggled as many do to put food on the table, but the love is there from the beginning and remains throughout his life. He will never fully leave the warmth of this family.

* * * * *

And that was as far as I got one Sunday morning in the fall of 2006 before the shift that changed my narrative tone from third-person to first and I typed out the words, "*I am born, David Henry Thoreau, in this American town, in this place called Concord.*" I thought to myself '*No, it can't be him. It can't possibly be him,*' even though I had been told back in January that year that I should prepare myself because in the fall my communication with Thoreau would begin.

That was on January 28, 2006 during a psychic reading that I had at Angelica of the Angels, a new age shop in the downtown pedestrian mall in Salem, Massachusetts, where I had been going for years in search of spiritual guidance. In the past my readings there were always with George Fraggos, who was co-owner of the store, along with Rev. Barbara Szafranski, his partner in business and life. George was the man I referred to in my book, *Honor in Concord*, as my favorite Salem Psychic, but on that day I had my first reading with Rev. Barbara. There were no preliminaries, no blessings, no prayers or preparations, in the way there had always been with George, at least none that I could see. Rev. Barbara's style was much more casual and I was surprised at how quickly she connected and at how accurately she described the events that had transpired three days before in my apartment in Cambridge, Massachusetts.

On January 25, 2006, the afternoon before the night that would mark the one year anniversary of my mother's passing, I was standing in my dining room in Cambridge in front of the built-in china cabinet shelves where I had placed photos of both of my parents and my grandmother, all who had passed during the prior few years, along with other objects that held some meaningful connection to them. It had become a sacred space in my home, where I often stood when I wanted to remember or to try to connect with them. That day as I stood there attempting to psychically connect to my mother in the way I had done many times during the past year, and as I reached for the photo of her that I planned to set near a candle on the dining room table that I would later light as a way to commemorate the one year anniversary of her passing, I suddenly found myself at first talking to and then seeing an image of my mentor, famed Thoreau scholar, Bradley P. Dean, Ph.D. I had not seen nor spoken to Brad since the annual gathering of the Thoreau Society in Concord, Massachusetts the previous July, and since I had not been to the Thoreau Society website recently and rarely spoke to other Thoreau Society members unless I ran into them at some event in Concord, I had no idea until that moment that Brad also had died.

I had been taught a long time ago by my mother who had lived her life in denial of her own psychic abilities to deny my own reality every time an event such as this one occurred, so my reaction to the exchange that took place that day between Brad and I was to quickly dismiss it. I told myself I was making it up. I told myself it couldn't possibly be so. I couldn't be talking to Brad in the way I had learned to talk to my Mom and Dad since their passing. Brad wasn't dead. He couldn't possibly be dead, and I so wanted to believe that. I set the candle and the picture of my mother on the dining room table and then headed into Boston to the law firm where I worked as a word processor on the evening shift and I acted as if that moment with Brad hadn't happened at all. Then a few hours later, while searching on the internet for an obituary for a neighbor who had recently passed, I found myself reading an obituary for Brad and learning (officially for the first time) about his sudden death from a heart attack at his home in Indiana, eleven days before.

As I read those words I knew that what had happened in my apartment in Cambridge that afternoon was real. Brad Dean was declared dead on January 14, 2006 in Bloomington, Indiana and yet I had seen him and spoken to him in Cambridge, Massachusetts in the afternoon of January 25, 2006. That is a fact. That is what happened. And with that revelation it was all I could do to maintain my composure as I looked at his face in the photograph on the monitor, read and reread his obituary and tried to make sense of it all. This handsome, dynamic, youthful-looking man who had so much to live for and so much to give had passed just three weeks before he had reached his 52nd birthday.

It didn't seem possible and it just wasn't fair and as I struggled to hold myself together emotionally, I became aware that Brad was once again there with me, this time in that law firm in Boston. I couldn't see him but I could sense him there and sense the urgency with which he wanted to speak to me, but given my surroundings, sitting at my desk with a coworker seated in the cubicle next to mine and several of the lawyers still lingering about after five o'clock, I knew whatever it was he wanted to say to me was going to have to wait. I managed to tell him this, through thoughts not words, and I promised we would talk later, when I was once again at home. That was my plan anyway, but by the time I returned home to Cambridge that evening after midnight the painful reality of the situation had begun to sink in. Brad was dead and I would never see him again, not in the way he was before anyway, and with that thought, and there in the privacy of my own home, I could no longer hold myself together. I folded up into a corner of the sofa and I wept, and in that state there was no way I could connect with him and hear what it was he wanted to say to me. All I could do at that point was cry.

* * *

The first time I saw Brad was at the annual gathering in the summer of 2002, when he entered the auditorium at the Masonic Temple in Concord after the lecture had already begun and caused enough of a distraction for the audience that the presenter paused to acknowledge his entrance. This was Bradley P. Dean, Ph.D., after all, the man who had made himself famous by editing and publishing Thoreau's unfinished manuscripts and who in 1996, upon the publication of the book, *Faith in a Seed*, had been invited to the White House to meet then Vice President, Al Gore. This was the man who in 2001 had published Thoreau's *Wild Fruits* and who was then currently at work on a collection of Thoreau's correspondence with H.G.O. Blake that would be published in 2004 under the title *Letters To A Spiritual Seeker*. I didn't know all this about Brad that day, but I learned it soon after when I had gone looking for all the information I could find about him.

We met for the first time at Lesley University in Cambridge the following February, after he had accepted my invitation to serve as advisor to me on the graduate program I had entered into there.

5

The focus of my independent study was to be "the Concord writers" and in the applicant's statement I had written for the program I had referred to myself as a "spiritual seeker". That phrase meant something to Brad because he told me during that February meeting that I had inspired the title for his third book. He also told me that day that the book that I was then writing, published in 2008 as *Honor in Concord: Seeking Spirit in Literary Concord*, segments of which he had read as part of my Lesley University application package, was the kind of book that he also wanted to write, but he had quickly assured me that with all the other projects he was engaged in he would have no time for that.

It seems clear to me now looking back that there were many ways that Brad and I connected that day, but at the time I was as insecure as I had always been. I was still struggling to gain some kind of recognition for the writing I had done and for the knowledge I had of the literary history of Concord. Brad was the one with all of the confidence and all the accomplishments. I felt intimidated by him and at the same time I felt drawn to him.

The graduate program at Lesley turned out to be a one semester thing for me, so we only saw each other at the annual gatherings for the next few years. We would speak only briefly, just long enough to say hello and for me to fill him in on the progress, or the lack of progress, I was making with my writing, no matter how awkward or uncomfortable those conversations often were for me. I was convinced that I was incapable of doing the kind of work that Brad and the other members of The Thoreau Society had done and yet I persisted. I was following my instincts and acting on an intuition that told me that I needed to stay in contact with Brad, and as I did, I was only consciously aware of two things. The first was simply that I wanted him to be my friend and the second was that, when it came to the books I wanted to write about the writers of Concord, in particular, Thoreau, I wanted Brad to help me.

That was what I said to him when I saw him on January 25, 2006, eleven days after he had passed at his home in Indiana and six months after July 2005 when I had last seen him at the Thoreau Society annual gathering in Concord. I said, "*I wanted you to help me. I wanted you to be my friend,*" and he replied in a rush of words, or I might better say thoughts that issued from him to me in that moment, which began with an apology for the way things had been left between us at the annual gathering the previous summer.

We had ended on a bad note. Somehow the tension between us that I was always determined to deny was there had reached culmination and the game we had been playing for the past three gatherings was over. Brad was tired of our brief encounters that always ended with me walking away from him, but on that last day when I saw him in Concord he was the one who walked away from me.

We were among a handful of people who had arrived early for the keynote address at First Parish Church in Concord that day. I was alone writing in my journal when Brad walked up the aisle past the pew where I was sitting and, once at the front of the church, stopped abruptly and turned to look at me, finally catching my eye in just the right way. This was the same church where a year later the urn containing his ashes would be placed in nearly the same spot where he then stood, and if I had the ability to turn back time I would choose that moment when he looked into my eyes and I would steadily and confidently return his gaze. I would welcome the opportunity for an honest exchange between us for perhaps the first time. Maybe then, together, we would have been able to figure out what it was that was going on between us.

This wasn't about a surface attraction or an affair that we might have but never did engage in. Brad and I had been drawn together for a purpose but on that day neither of us could have imagined what that purpose was or what the circumstances would be that would bring it about, and whatever it was that Brad wanted to say to me in that moment was left unsaid. I simply wasn't ready for the conversation that he and I needed to have so I averted his gaze by burying my face in the pages of my journal and he walked away. That was the last time I saw Brad - well, the last time until after his death - but then of course Brad didn't die, not really, because no one, none of us ever does.

I had learned that years before by the many times I had either received messages from or actually encountered individuals after they had died. From 1980 to 1984, while finishing my bachelor's degree at Michigan State University, I had worked full-time for an oncologist in Lansing, Michigan, handling medical insurance matters for his terminally ill patients. I had grown fond of many of those people who were experiencing the final phase of their lives at that time and many of them had visited me after their deaths, simply to express their thanks to me and to bid me farewell.

There were other times, too, throughout my life when I had been visited by individuals soon after their deaths. In one case, it was the father of a woman I worked with whose grief over his passing, and within a short time the passing of her brother, had been eased by a book by psychic, George Anderson that I had given her to read. Her father had simply wanted to thank me for helping her through her enormous grief. I was also visited by my Godfather three days before my father had called me to share the news of his best friend's death. A few years later, I had an incredible encounter with my father during his passing, although it was taking place in Michigan, many hundreds of miles away from where I was in Massachusetts.

In his book, *Glimpses of Eternity* (2009), Dr. Raymond Moody, who in 1975 had coined the term *"near death experience"*, coined the term *"shared death experience"* to describe experiences like the one I had with my father at the end of his life. I had known that his death would come soon but I was not aware that he was in the process of dying when during a meditation I asked to be shown what it was he would see as he crossed over. I was soon drawn into a place where I experienced the most intense feeling of love I have ever felt and where I saw my father, not as an old man with one leg dying in his nursing home bed, but as a young man with his body restored, running at full speed up a hillside to where those who loved him were waiting to welcome him.

When I realized that what I was seeing was actually taking place I called out *"Dad, are you going?"* and when I did my father turned and came quickly towards me and just at that moment my telephone rang. I heard nothing but buzzing the first time I picked it up, evidently his energies had interfered with the electricity in the house, but a few minutes later the phone rang again. That time I heard my mother telling me that the nursing home had called to let her know he was getting ready to pass. In my excitement I replied, *"I know! I just saw him!"* In fact, I had seen him, and by calling out to him in the way that I had I had brought him back. As the family in Michigan gathered around his bedside that night to say their farewells his vital signs improved. He was back in that aged body again and it would be another 24 hours before he finally passed on.

I remember remarking to Brad one time after my father's passing, *"Oh, it's only death..."* and as I walked away I heard him call out to me, *"I know!"* I realize now all these years later that Brad really did understand what I understood about the reality of spirit and of the continuation of life after death. He had even addressed it in some of the articles he had written just before he passed, highlighting the ways in which Thoreau understood this, too, including the teaching notes he had written for *Life with Principle*, a DVD program produced by The Thoreau Society, and in an essay that was published posthumously in 2007 in a book entitled, *American Wilderness: A New History* edited by Michael Lewis. He also took part in visionary, Connie Baxter Marlow's *American Evolution* film series, and was the keynote speaker at the seminar she hosted in Aspen, Colorado in June 2005. In all of those cases, Brad discussed what is known as the "contact passage" in which Thoreau describes the revelatory experience he had atop Mt. Katahdin in Maine in 1846. Brad points out in clear terms how Thoreau's description of his experience on Mt. Katahdin demonstrates his belief that we are more than our physical bodies and that we do survive physical death.

While most Thoreauvians view Thoreau as a naturalist and focus primarily on what they believe to be his political views, Brad had dared to closely consider the passages in Thoreau's work that pointed to his deep understanding of spirit. This was a revelation to me when I discovered it. How vague and limited my own understanding of Thoreau's beliefs were at the time this all began. Although I had spent years reading about his life in Concord, I had not paid close enough attention to Thoreau's words. For over 20 years I had done my spiritual seeking within the new age community and I kept that separate and apart from my literary pursuits, but all of that began to change for me on January 25, 2006.

After the apologies that Brad and I exchanged that day in my dining room in Cambridge I turned to see an image of him a few feet away from me and I watched as he placed his hands together above his head in a "V" formation and then drew them down in front of

9

him. I wasn't sure exactly what he was doing at the time and I joked later that it looked like some kind of Namaste greeting but during the reading with Rev. Barbara at Angelica of the Angels in Salem three days later, after quickly connecting with Brad and describing his "not so small nose" and what she thought at first were lines but what I knew was the shape of his mustache as it ran along the sides of his mouth, I watched with awe and amusement as she made that same "V" formation with her own hands that I had seen him do and drew it down in front of her in the same way he had done. Rev. Barbara told me Brad was drawing his energy down to me and further igniting for me the fire that was there inside of me already, the one that had led me to Concord and to the transcendentalists in the first place. Brad was telling me that he would continue to work with me now from spirit just as he had in life, and, as that first reading with Rev. Barbara continued, I was told to prepare myself because in the fall Thoreau would begin working with me, too.

Thoreau came into the reading that day soon after I asked the question I felt those who knew Brad and understood the strength of his devotion to Thoreau would most want to ask. I asked, "*Has he met Henry?*" and, as soon as I asked the question, I felt another energy come into the room. Rev. Barbara's answer was, "*Yes, they have been batting words around,*" and, before I had explained to her that the Henry I had asked about was Henry David Thoreau, the writer who was famous for living in the cabin at Walden Pond, she described him as a man with wavy brown hair, a thin face and large nose who spoke of the closeness of the bond he had with Brad and the fondness he expressed towards me.

Rev. Barbara went on to reveal the ways in which Brad would, in her words, "*light my bulb*" and the manner in which Brad and Henry would begin to convey information to me that would later make up the content of this book. She said there would be pages of text appearing in front of me in dreams and I would awaken with information that I would need to write down. Without any prior knowledge of Brad's expertise on the computer, or of my own as a word processor, Rev. Barbara drew a computer monitor and described how she could see the words moving swiftly across the screen. She told me that this process would begin in November because I would need time before then to finish the book I was already writing. That book was what I later published as *Honor in*

Concord, and it was the book that Brad had read a segment of before he passed, the one he had said was the kind of book he wanted to write. The subtitle, *Seeking Spirit in Literary Concord,* is my homage to Brad's use of the phrase spiritual seeker and the book is dedicated to him.

There were two other readings with Rev. Barbara that followed that initial one in January. There was one in May before the annual gathering that year and one that came soon after. In May they offered me support for a decision I had made to move back to Concord. Well, it was actually a townhouse in a duplex just over the town line into Bedford, and I would live there for three years before finally establishing myself in Concord proper again. It was there in that place with the Bedford address that most of the material for this book was received, and where the communications with Thoreau began that Sunday afternoon while I was sitting at the computer and attempting to type up some of the notes I had written upon waking many mornings in the prior weeks. After recording those initial notes I began writing the third-person segment that suddenly transitioned into first-person with the words "*I am born David Henry Thoreau.*"

One day early on in the transmissions I was given a statement in response to my own concerns about how this book would be perceived and how I myself would be regarded. That statement appears on the back cover of this book and here.

> Whether this work is channeled or simply inspired little matters for the depth of information and wisdom it contains. Those who read it are unlikely to look at Thoreau in the same way again. In *The Thoreau Whisperer*, the relevance of his message in our lives has never been more evident. It is a message that is as timeless, ageless and as infinite as we are. It is the message of the soul.

This experience has changed my life in many ways. First, and probably foremost, it has forced me to come to terms with a gift that I have had since childhood of being able to see and communicate with those who are in spirit and it has convinced me once and for all that life does continue after physical death.

As I stated on my website early on in this process: *"All who ever were still are and always will be."* I honestly and wholeheartedly believe that.

THE MESSENGER

Chapter Two
Biography

...because the truest of all truths will be found in the words of Thoreau.

Henry David Thoreau was born in Concord, Massachusetts on July 12, 1817. He was the third of four children of John Thoreau and Cynthia Dunbar. Other than the first few years of his life, Thoreau spent his entire life living in Concord. He said of it, "*I have never got over my surprise that I should have been born into the most estimable place in all the world, and in the very nick of time, too.*"[2]

There are few men who live who achieve the greatness of this man known as Henry David Thoreau. It was not seen or known within the course of his life, but in the words that survived him and that have been read and reflected upon by so many. That is because there is within each of his observations of the world the purest truth and it is a truth that stems from his understanding of spirit.

This man in his life was not so well adept, that is if we judge him in the common way that humans are often judged, by their physical appearance or their material accomplishments, but what of their moral accomplishments? What of the factor of honor and integrity in their lives? What of the deepest and most important ties that bind us to our source and to each other? What of spirit? In this regard, we cannot overestimate Thoreau's value because of the

---

[2] From Thoreau's Journal, December 5, 1856.

strength and power of his words, because the truest of all truths will be found in the words of Thoreau.

For those who have never read Thoreau's work and who consider it best left in the hands of the academics, I encourage you to read him for when you do you will find that the heart of his message is a simple one. Do with less, want for less, because when you are in touch with your truest self you will see that you have all that you need and that all that you are is permanent and everlasting. The spirit in you does not wear down the way the body wears down. It does not lose color or diminish in strength. It stays strong and steady and when the body reaches its end the spirit casts itself back into the light from whence it came where it is renewed and reinvigorated and sets out to create again.

Henry David Thoreau attended Harvard College in Cambridge from 1833-1837. While there he read the essay Ralph Waldo Emerson called, *Nature*. It was an essay that described a philosophy called transcendentalism[3] and to Thoreau it was an articulation of his own knowledge and experience. It was through the purity and truth in nature that Thoreau had first felt the stirrings of his own soul.

After returning to Concord in 1837, Thoreau met Emerson for the first time and that meeting between Emerson, who was a sage at 34 and Thoreau, who was then only 20, marked the beginning of an extraordinary association. It was Emerson who recommended Thoreau keep a journal; it was Emerson who encouraged Thoreau to write and who helped to get his early essays and poems placed in the publication called *The Dial*; and it was Emerson who gave Thoreau permission to build a cabin on a piece of land that he owned at Walden Pond.

Thoreau's masterpiece, *Walden or Life in the Woods*, was published in 1854, and was enough to establish him as a

---

[3] Transcendentalism is a philosophy that evolved from the writings of German philosopher, Immanuel Kant, who favored intuition over reason as a method for determining an ultimate truth that he believed was innate and intuitively understood by man. At its base, Transcendentalism is the belief that we are not merely physical beings, we are spirit.

writer during his lifetime. In the last few years of his life he was frequently visited by those who had read *Walden* and wished to know the author. In addition to *Walden*, and his extensive journals that are felt by some to be his greatest accomplishment, Thoreau wrote other books, poems and essays and delivered lectures on the issues of his day. His best known essay, *Civil Disobedience*, was inspired by a dispute over taxes that led to a night in the Concord jail. He also wrote essays and spoke out powerfully for the abolition of slavery and against the government that supported it; he spoke out for the rights of the individual over the demands of any government because he felt the only laws that should govern any man were the divine laws; and he spoke of the ability of man to intuit his own right actions through his conscience, which is a direct connection to the divine.

Thoreau passed into spirit on May 6, 1862, another victim of tuberculosis, or what was called consumption, the disease that had taken the lives of so many in the 19th century, and yet two centuries later, his words, his wisdom and his spirit endure.

* * *

That biographical sketch of Thoreau has been running on my website (www.theconcordwriter.com) since 2008, and as I consider the question of whether or not it is necessary to know about the writer in order to better understand or appreciate his words, I ask myself, how much more than that do we need to know about Thoreau in order to read and understand his message?

Thoreau is well aware of the thousands of books that have been written about him since his death, and of the way those books have influenced people's views of him. There have been hundreds of biographies written about him, most by those who never knew him at all and few of them do him any kind of justice. Still they are there and available for anyone who wishes to read them. The latest addition is *Henry David Thoreau: A Life* by Laura Dassow Walls (2017), but the standards that I have always relied on are Walter Harding's, *The Days of Henry Thoreau* (1962) and Henry Seidel Canby's *Thoreau* (1939). The one that was remembered fondly by

Brad as the book that opened him up to Thoreau was Joseph Wood Krutch's *Henry David Thoreau* (1948). For the purpose of this book, beyond the few key facts I offer about Thoreau's life, mostly in the footnotes I provide, we will rely on the biographical information that Thoreau shares within the text of the channeled materials.

As a transcendentalist, Thoreau believed in establishing a direct connection with the divine. He believes in the same style of direct relation to the written word. If you can read and comprehend words you can understand his message, without the aid of anyone else, particularly those who you encounter in the realms of so-called higher education. He said to me early on and with much enthusiasm, *"Remind them they need only themselves and their own eyes and their own minds to read and comprehend my thoughts."*

* * *

Chapter Three
The First Transmission

"I strive to see and know more than these people of the village do."

This chapter contains the full text of the original transmission I received from Thoreau one Sunday morning in November 2006. I have made editorial changes here and with the other transmissions that follow, not of content but more of grammar and format, as this process of transcribing the words that came through was not always smooth or perfectly grammatical. I have also taken steps to remove repetitions as there were many that occurred during the years when the transmissions were most frequent. There are, however, several key points that he returns to throughout the transmissions.

I would also like to note that although I use the word channeled to describe the process of communication engaged in and the materials received, the actual method of communication was more like automatic writing. I would sit down at my computer, close my eyes, spend a minute or two connecting and then, with eyes still closed, type out the words that were transmitted to me. It was like the transcription work I have made a living doing for years except in this case there was no tape playing, just a stream of words and ideas that flowed into my mind from another source. At no time in this process was I ever required to leave my body in order for Thoreau or anyone else in spirit to step in.

I feel privileged to have known Brad Dean and to have come together with him in the way that we have in order to bring Thoreau's message to light again at this time. I experience Thoreau as a gentle, kind but determined spirit, whose humor and wisdom seem to be fully intact, and I find Brad as real and alive as he was in life, humorous, difficult at times but in his actions toward me always thoughtful and kind. It has truly been an honor for me to engage in this collaboration with both of them.

Lastly, as we proceed let me repeat, there is no way for me to convince any of you who venture to read this book that the words it contains do in fact originate with the spirit of the man who once lived a life as Henry David Thoreau, but after a lifetime of experiences that do not fit into any framework of what is commonly considered normal, I am left to conclude that they do. I also believe it is only a matter of time now before science proves both the survival of consciousness after physical death and that communication between the physical and the spiritual worlds has occurred. The ramifications of such revelations will be considerable.

THE FIRST TRANSMISSION

As received in November 2006

I am born, David Henry Thoreau[4], in this American town, in this place called Concord. There is a history here already, history of the men who came here from Europe to settle this town in 1635, men like the Reverend Peter Bulkeley, who was the many times great-grandfather of Ralph Waldo Emerson, the man who would be remembered as "God" in Concord,[5] and then there would be me, Henry. I am a poor physical relic of a man, compared to other men in the town. My awkward features, described so well and with brutal honesty by Hawthorne[6], help to shape the man I become. I do not fit, as other men fit into the role of husband, father or provider. Women do not look at me with fond and loving eyes, the way they look at men like my brother, John, or Waldo's brother, Charles, men with fine features, better manners and more compliant natures than my own. The words of Elizabeth Hoar, who would have become Charles' wife, had he lived, and who became his wife through her devotion to him in spirit, captured the general feeling of the women of the town towards me, "*I would no sooner take Henry's arm, than to take hold of the limb of a tree...*"[7]

There is a boldness to me, a rugged truth that they are unable to relate to. They want their fine linens, fine dresses, fine homes, and comfortable surroundings. I bristle at the thought of their complacency. Is there not more to be learned and lived than that which takes place cradling a child round the fire - perpetuating more and more life and yielding our own to the propulsion of that effort - rather than to stall the process long enough to reflect and question, where is the value in life anyway?

---

[4] At his birth on July 12, 1817, Thoreau was named David Henry Thoreau. He was an adult when he chose to reverse the order of his name to Henry David.

[5] This reference is to the book, *God in Concord* by Richard G. Geldard (1998).

[6] In his journal entry dated September 1, 1842, Nathaniel Hawthorne wrote of Thoreau, "*He is as ugly as sin, long-nosed, queer-mouthed, and with uncouth and somewhat rustic, although courteous manners, corresponding very well with such an exterior. But his ugliness is of an honest and agreeable fashion, and becomes him much better than beauty.*"

[7] Elizabeth Hoar is quoted as having said, "*One would as soon think of taking the arm of an elm-tree as Henry's.*" and adding "*I love Henry, but I can never like him.*"

I strive to see and know more than these people of the village do. They want to follow the narrow path, the path that leads to their familiar homes, to interact with their familiar friends in familiar conversation on topics they already know, and read stories that reinforce and glorify their style of life. Tea served in a fine china cup at the tea house in Concord is the same to me as the tea served in a china cup in a fine salon of Paris, whereas the tea I drink that is prepared from the waters of Walden Pond, and sipped slowly while sitting at the edge of the pond and taking in the still silence of a winter morning, that is tea worth drinking.

I do not wish to get ahead of myself by mentioning too soon this place I am so famous for frequenting. It is true that I did live there for two years, two months and two days, but my earliest memory of the pond comes in a ride taken four years after my birth, when my family returned to Concord, after living a few years away in Chelmsford and Boston. And I remember sitting on the buckboard of that carriage and looking out at the glistening blue waters of the pond as the carriage passed. If it is true that many people experience certain moments in their early lives that foreshadow major events in their lives to come, I would say this was the moment for me, as although just a small child then, I was entranced by the natural beauty of that place, and there was something there that called to me, and as I continue to witness it, it seems that it still calls out to those who can hear it.

But I will get to the story of the pond later. For now, it is important to understand how I began and why I became the man I became. In anyone's life, it is worthwhile to stop long enough to remember the child they once were, so I will remember it now.

Being born in what was my grandmother's widow's thirds of the Minot House on the old Virginia Road in Concord, July 12, 1817. My father was John Thoreau II, born October 6, 1787, son of immigrant John Thoreau, born 1754, who immigrated to New England from the Isle of Jersey in 1773, and operated a business at Long Wharf and later on King Street, now State Street in downtown Boston. In 1781, he married my grandmother, Jane Burns, who was daughter to Scotsman, Peter Burns and Sarah

22

Orrok, who hailed from Massachusetts Quaker stock. Together they had eight children, among them my father, John Thoreau II, and my Aunts, Maria and Jane. My mother was born Cynthia Dunbar in Keene, NH on May 23, 1787. Her father, my grandfather, the Reverend Asa Dunbar, was born in Bridgewater, MA in 1745 and died in 1787 at age 42, leaving his wife, Mary Jones Dunbar widowed at 39. She later married Captain Jonas Minot, and together they lived in his house on Virginia Road. After his death in 1813, my grandmother was given the widow's thirds of the home from his estate, and it is in this sector of the home on Virginia Road that I was born.

My parents had come to live at the Virginia Road house of my grandmother, bringing with them their eldest child, a daughter, my sister, Helen, soon to be 5 years old, and a son, my brother John, then 3 years old. My presence in the house could only have added to the congestion and the confusion of the place, and to my father's sense of urgency at finding another occupation and a place for his blossoming family to live. The products of the farm land then produced food for the family, but little profits. By 1818, he had moved us, his family, to Chelmsford, where he ran a mercantile business. There was a brief return to Concord in 1819 and then we were on to Boston where we lived at Pinckney Square on Beacon Hill and father's business in Boston was a mild success. It is interesting to note that the place where we lived on Pinckney Street on Beacon Hill was but a short distance from the home where Waldo's family had moved in 1815, two years before my birth and two years before Waldo's entrance into university at Cambridge. He was a young man of fourteen at the time when he began his studies at Harvard College, a place I would also attend, sixteen years later.

I remember little of those days in Boston, being so young then, but the closeness of everything, and the combination of smells that never seemed pleasing. I remember the constant attention I had then from my mother and my sister, Helen, as well as my aunts who were frequent guests in our home then. They were critical figures who helped form the conditions of my life. An abundance of feminine love and attention, a more restrained and cautious love from my father, and I had the companionship of my brother, John.

They would later emphasize the differences between John and me, how he was more refined, well mannered and more truthful than me. There they may have been wrong unless by truthful they were referring to his ability to conform to their expectations of what a man should be, but I knew who John was, as a boy and later as a man. He was my brother and my best friend, and I will concede his possession of the fine graceful ways that were lacking in me, but I will never grant that he did not share the wildness in me. We spent our lives together exploring the natural settings in Concord.

Arriving in town that day in 1823, we moved first into the home shared by my aunts on Monument Street, the home that now-a-days makes up part of the Colonial Inn. There I grew from age 4 to 7. I attended public school in Concord, spent a brief time at Miss Phoebe Wheeler's school for girls, where my mother had sent my brother, John and me to continue our learning after the public school had temporarily closed; and at the Concord Academy, where my teacher was Phineas Allen.[8]

In 1833, I entered Harvard College in Cambridge, living in Hollis Hall. My roommate, Charles Stearns Wheeler, who had been raised in nearby Lincoln, was a good friend. Those were years of some enjoyment, but most difficulty. I could not see the value of much of the teaching, or more so sometimes enjoyed the books, but not the instructors.

My parents were not wealthy, so their efforts to put me through this school were of no short measure. These were the efforts of a loving family toward their son in shoring up what they hoped would be a bright future for me. I am afraid I disappointed them later by my choice of occupation.

---

[8] Phineas Allen is credited as the instructor who prepared Thoreau for entry into Harvard College.

Teaching in a classroom setting was not something that I enjoyed. I disagreed with the accepted methods of instruction and of corporal punishment used in order to keep a student in line. I myself had endured such treatment as a child, and saw no value in such brutality. At the same time, I lacked the ease and comfort with teaching that my brother displayed, so again he was the favored instructor during the years we taught at the Concord Academy. He had a gentle, reassuring manner with the students that I could also see and admire. My manner by contrast, was not so much brutish, as it was reserved, reserved at least until I brought the students outside and we could move about freely, laughing and playing, while learning through first hand observations. The young boys in particular were a sheer pleasure to me, as they were freer than most of the girls, except perhaps for the charming Louisa May[9], the one I thought the brightest and liveliest of Bronson's brood of women. She was my student for a short time there at the academy, and as I was friend to her father, and frequent guest at her home, I had the opportunity to study her up close and early recognized her as the wisest of women that she would become. She was not restrained, not held back and not caught up in viewing herself through the same single lens that other women would view their lives. She was an original and as I am cast from the same original foundation, I found her uniquely refreshing. She too had admired the wildness in me.

RALPH WALDO EMERSON

I had read Waldo's[10] book, *Nature*[11], as I lie on the bed in my room at Harvard College. At last a book that focused on nature, a subject most dear to me, and yet I was not prepared for the words that flowed from this man. For the first time someone had captured the essence of what nature had always been to me. There in nature lay the truth to our own divinity. There within the spirit of nature, was our own spirit, our own inner workings that would

---

[9] Here he is referring to author, Louisa May Alcott (1832-1888), and to her father, transcendentalist, Amos Bronson Alcott (1799-1888).

[10] Ralph Waldo Emerson is referred to by Thoreau as Waldo throughout the transmissions.

[11] *Nature*, written by Ralph Waldo Emerson and published in 1836 became the manifesto for the transcendentalist movement.

lead to the greatest of revelations in me. This was the book that changed my life, the book that opened my eyes to what life could be. I never looked at life the same way again after reading that book, and I never again felt myself deficient in any way for lacking the calling for a traditional life that other men, even Waldo himself, would fall prey to. I embraced my liberty in a new way, and understood myself better than I ever had before.

This was the turning point in my life. This was the man who stepped in and helped to shape my life. I give him credit now that I did not fully give him then. I was a young man, full of myself and my own thoughts and ambitions, and he was considerably older than I and wiser. He had been able to bridge that gap between youthful ambition, joyful revelation and the dream of freedom, and the life of a mature man, a family man, a man respected in his community. I was not respected in my community, but felt no sense of loss at that lack of respect. There was no one there, save perhaps Waldo himself, whose respect I required. And there was a falling out with him, at a certain point, perhaps not unexpected, because at first he was like a father to me, feeding me with the knowledge that I longed for but never received from my own father, who was a worthwhile but simple and not so well educated man. But as with any father and son there comes a time when a son must break free, when the words of the father become more oppressive than inspiring, and that is what happened with Waldo and me.

But let there be no mistake, Waldo Emerson was a hero to me. They say that I spoke like him, that I mimicked him, and that the words I later wrote were born of him. It is true only in part that we seek to emulate those we most admire, but he was more a stepping stone to my own revelation and experience of life. He relished his role as a grand wise man, sitting comfortably in his fine home, and handing out his wisdom to those who came round. I do not deny him his grandeur. He was a great and fine man. I do deny that I was in any sense a copy of him. Look at our lives. Where do you see a similarity? Look at our works, there is no similarity beyond the content of the message that yes, we did share.

But our experience of that truth was far different. You can see only so much from your position on that high thrown, but I preferred to walk the path in the woodland, to see nature firsthand and to sense and feel the spirit that was there within nature and is there within me. I do not know if Waldo ever truly felt the spirit he wrote and so often spoke about.

I remember with fondness the day I first met him. It was the sister of Waldo's wife, Lidian Jackson, a woman named Lucy Brown of Plymouth, who had arranged for the introduction. I had maintained my composure, but felt a certain amount of nervousness at the prospect of meeting this man. I had sat for a few minutes unaccompanied in his study, admiring the many volumes of books that lined the shelves. Soon Waldo entered the room and with a wide smile took my hand in introduction, and we remained there in his study for the ensuing hours, discussing at length the principles outlined in his book, but also discussing details of our lives that I suspect he discussed with few of the other young men who came to meet him.

There are people whom we meet in life who we feel we may have either known before, or who we feel we were somehow destined to meet. It was certainly true for me that day and I suspect for Waldo it was true as well. There was something unique in our meeting, something at work that was larger than our own personal cause and concerns, and certainly that has proved to be true as all these years later, our names are inextricably linked. We can think of many men throughout history whose lives come together for the import of their shared mission, not for the benefit of themselves, but for the benefit of those others who will be impacted by the experiences or the art work or the stories that are told and retold about the times they spent together. There were Socrates and Plato, Lewis and Clark, and even musicians, Lennon and McCartney, but for this time in the mid 19th century, there was Waldo and me.

I left there that day, filled with the excitement of the revelations we had shared. Here in Waldo was a man who understood the spiritual dimension in life. He was descended from a long line of ministers, but this inner awareness, forced to the surface at the crisis in faith he had suffered upon the death of his first wife,[12] proved to be a more powerful truth than any that was presented through a typical interpretation of the Bible.

We became friends that day, and I returned to the Emerson's home many times, until I was invited to stay there, and to earn my keep by acting as handyman around the house and by watching out for his wife, Lidian, and their children during Waldo's long absences. This was an opportunity for me to break from the familiar comfort of my family's home and I found a second family for myself with the Emersons. Their children, Wallie, Ellen and Edith, and later Edward were delightful, and as I was closer to them in energy than their father, they experienced me as a wise, yet playful older brother and I experienced with them the joyful wealth of the spirits of children, a precious commodity and one that is so soon and so often sacrificed to the mundane detail of physical life.

I cherish my memories of those times, of those precious children, and of the lovely and gracious Lidian, who I saw as sister rather than lover, and whom I did love with a spiritual more than romantic love. It is an intrigue to me that there are those who speculate on an affair between the two of us. It would have been more as a mother molesting her eldest child, as we were in fact of such a long age gap. It is impossible at times to understand the dynamics between two people when viewed from a distant and future place. To make love to a woman who was wife to a friend would have been then and I believe in spite of all the generations who have come and gone since and all the changes in mores, would still be considered the highest form of betrayal. I would not have betrayed my friend, Waldo, in that way, yet I had seen no reason why not to express my feelings to Lidian and that I did in several letters. I regret this in some ways, as I believe they caused

---

[12] Ellen Louisa Tucker (1811-1831) was 16 when she met Ralph Waldo Emerson, 18 when they married and 19 when she passed from tuberculosis on February 8, 1831. Emerson, who was deeply in love with Ellen, later gave the daughter he had with his second wife, Lydia (Lidian) Jackson Emerson (1802-1892), the name Ellen Tucker Emerson (1839-1909).

her some distress rather than comfort and they are the source of the speculation that continues.

WOMEN & SEXUALITY

I was not a man as most men are men. I did not have the same physical appetite for women that they do. The only love that ever appealed to me was the higher love, the bond that is spiritual and that exists for ever and always, but I was not so intrigued by the physical aspects of love on the earth. Perhaps it was an innate aestheticism. There was something so utterly vulgar in the act of sexual intercourse that I couldn't get past. I remember the reaction I received from Ellery[13] one day when we discussed this topic. I did not see what was so appealing in the perfumed and powdered women who would sometimes come around us. I did not feel enticed by them, I did not feel drawn to them, did not want to touch or smell or defile them in any way, as it seemed to me other men longed to do. If they could attract me with their beauty and grace and I could relate it to a higher vibration, I could allow myself to love, but rarely, if ever, to lust.

I did not feel the same inhibitions toward men. My interactions with them were more smoothly correspondent. I do not admit an affinity for them, in a physical or sexual way, just a comfort with them and affinity for their wilder natures. I would thrill in the time spent with some of my male friends and never experienced the same thrill in the company of women.

---

[13] William Ellery Channing II was the nephew of the Unitarian Minister of the same name. He was one of the many young men who gathered at the Emerson home and he and Thoreau became close friends. In 1873, eleven years after Thoreau's death, Ellery Channing published a biography of Thoreau entitled: *Thoreau: The Poet Naturalist*.

ELLEN SEWALL

There was Ellen Sewall[14], who so much has been written about. Ellen had been loved and wooed both by my brother, John, and by me, but she had ultimately turned down each of our marriage proposals. Ellen was a lovely girl when she first came to Concord. John and I took turns courting her, and I, as the younger and recognizably the less appealing of the two of us, had held back my affection, allowing for John's first pursuit.

To deny that there was a resultant tension between us would be to do a disservice to the truth of the story. Of course there was tension, not the least of which in July 1840 when John went to Plymouth to seek out her promise of marriage, and I was left at home to wonder what the outcome would be. I admit to having rejoiced at his failure and at the hope that she would instead marry me, but my proposal to her was also declined. Her father had stood in the way of her marriage to either my brother or me. He envisioned a better life for his daughter than he felt either John or I could provide for her, so she married a man who would one day be preacher and my brother and I went on as solitary souls.

Yet I remained in love with Ellen for the rest of my life and comforted myself in the belief that she had also loved me, but my love for her was an idealized, romantic and youthful love, as was whatever love she may have held for me, but the love she found in her life with her husband, that mean, coarse, physical love that I feared, had satisfied her more than my love ever could.

JOHN THOREAU, JR.

The initial tension between John and I over our shared admiration of Ellen after meeting her in July 1839 had dissipated quickly and

---

[14] Ellen Devereux Sewall (1822-1892) was the daughter of Edmund Q. and Caroline (Ward) Sewall. After refusing proposals from both Henry and John Thoreau, at the wish of her father, she married Rev. Joseph Osgood and had several children. Thoreau never married and was to say year's later that he had always loved Ellen. After her death, Ellen's daughter said that her mother had never forgotten Thoreau and that her father, Rev. Osgood had often wondered if his wife would have been happier had she married Thoreau and not him.

by August we were planning a trip together, a boating trip, in fact, that would become the basis of my first book, *A Week on the Concord and Merrimac Rivers*. I would look back at this time spent with my brother as a gift, not knowing at the time how early his short but perfect life would end.

I say he was perfect, because I remember him then, handsome, full of life, full of caring for people. He was well known in town, well loved by his family and well liked by friends. We could not believe the trouble that had befallen us when the lockjaw set in. Nor could he believe his grim fate. Why, Henry, why? He would ask me so desperately. I could give him no answer, but only give him reassurances, we do live on, I know we live on.

He died in my arms, a winter day. I felt and saw his spirit lift from him, a silvery mist that rose from the bed and hung there in the air momentarily as if saying a final farewell before dissipating. What a picture he must have seen of me sobbing over what was left of him, and at the same time buoyed by the awakening of the soul. *"Oh Henry, you were right,"* I could hear him say. *"I am still alive!"*

And then there were mother and father and Helen and Sophia crowding around, all of us in utter disbelief that he could leave us this way. Did he not understand how important he was to us, and how important he remained, although so much was to go on after he left. I often wondered if he was aware of the events of my life that transpired after his death, if he had witnessed Emerson's ascension or later my own.[15] All those days of life he had missed. And how would his life have been, living I expect as husband to a wife and father to his children. The name of Thoreau would have continued if John had continued, of this I am sure.

---

[15] It is ascension in status and accomplishments that Thoreau refers to here, and it appears to be another reference to Emerson's status as God in Concord, a notion that seems to both amuse and confound Thoreau.

THE GENTLE BOY [16]

There is the poem I wrote about the gentle boy. Yes, I loved the gentle boy, how could I not? He was so wise and fine, so delicate an expression of God, and I was enraptured by him. They call this homoerotic, but I call it simple passion for an expression of beauty in life that he was then. He enlivened something in me as no one had ever done before. I have said enough and that is sufficient.

CONCORD, MASSACHUSETTS

I would have no surer place in this world than the one I found in Concord. I said once that I considered myself blessed to be born in such an estimable place,[17] and still I look upon the town and regard it in the same way. There was then in my time and there remains today a quality to this town that is unmatched in other places. It is not through the people, although many are fine, but there is an undertow of energy that exists there in the downtown and extends out to the pond. Is it the events that transpired there that make Concord such a place or have the events transpired there because it was and is such a place? For me, it was and remains a place where nature exists in perfect majesty and sets the tone for that air of magic that permeates. I have heard it said that one day Concord will be a crystal city, a safe haven of retreat for those who flee the difficulties and the madness of the times. It was always for me a magical place.

I am a young man when I first advance out of the town for Cambridge. Living in a room at Harvard and attending classes there is a new adventure for me. There are many young men like myself, some with more serious drive than me. They envision great careers in law or politics, fine homes with wives and children.

---

[16] Thoreau's poem, *The Gentle Boy*, has often been cited as an indication of his homosexuality. Many say it was written about Ellen Sewall's younger brother, Edmund, but Thoreau's sister, Sophia, claimed it had been written about his brother, John.

[17] Thoreau wrote in his journal on December 5, 1856: "*I have never got over my surprise that I should have been born into the most estimable place in all the world, and in the very nick of time, too.*"

I am not a good student. I am more interested in my own pursuits than fulfilling any obligation to attain any good grade. Still, I make my way year after year until the course load is through and I am again released back to my family.

I return home an educated, but still unambitious man. I cannot find intrigue in a typical life. I look at the men and women of this town and feel foreign to them. I do not understand the motivation that demands that we take physical and emotional possession of each other, and bring forth new life. This commingling of souls seems foreign to me. It is for me and me alone that I seek the truth, and it is through me alone that I can find it. Any cohabitation or commingling of the kind I see around me seems to me to be taxing and stands in the way of an ultimate journey. That is how I see it, however wrong or misplaced that sentiment might be. It is not that others are impeded in their situations, as I myself might be in theirs. We are each to find our own ways, but I feel that for many they follow the traditional ways and ultimately find themselves regretful.

OUTCAST

So what then will I do with my life? That is the question that is put to me, often by my father and by other well meaning but predictable men of the town who are intoxicated by their status in life, their prominence and the respect bestowed upon them at the town meeting. I want more from my life but even I at that point cannot be sure what the more is. I receive a certain tolerance from my family but that tolerance is less so bestowed by the townspeople. These people, these citizens of the town, look upon me as an outcast, a wayward offspring of an otherwise respectable family. I look at myself I suppose as I always have, still as a child who wants only to frolic in the woods and not take on the responsibilities of life. I see those responsibilities as burden not benefit. I would rather live on nothing, than suffer one day's labor to provide one day's comfort for myself. I can live on little and therefore preserve my life energy for my own purposes.

There is so much to do in a day so much to learn. I am excited by each sunrise that a new day dawns for me to explore the universe that lies outside my door. That is truly the way I feel about it. They make fun of my ways, my lingering over the simplest and what is to them the most trivial of the operations of nature. Mrs. French recorded her conversation with Murray, the farmer, who complained to her at finding me studying the activities of the bullfrog one day for nearly the entire day. He thought I was wasting my time, but I stayed for as long as I needed to stay to take in every nuance of a life well lived. The life of the frogs seems to me as relevant as the life of a man, but men see themselves as superior in the universe and disrespect the other creatures. I never saw myself that way. Each of us is an integral part of the whole, and none should disrespect the actions of another, as long as they are right action, action that springs from the higher source.

* * *

Chapter Four
Believing

Why would Thoreau be talking to me?

For weeks after this first transmission I struggled with my own inability to believe that the words I was receiving had originated with Thoreau. I went over in my mind the things that Rev. Barbara had said to me during that first reading in Salem. I thought about the way she had imitated the gesture I had seen Brad make with his hands over his head and I thought about her explanation that he was drawing his energy down to me. I understood that by doing that Brad was helping to prepare me for when the communications with Thoreau would begin but now that they had begun I was having a hard time accepting it all. I wondered, if in fact it was Thoreau, how was it possible for me to hear him in this way and why me? Why would Thoreau be talking to me?

In an attempt to answer that question I asked myself and then answered the following: Do you believe that we live on after physical death? My answer was yes. Do you believe it is possible for those who occupy physical bodies to communicate with those who do not? My answer was yes. Do you have the ability to connect to spirit and to receive those transmissions? Again, my answer was yes. It seemed a logical conclusion then that this could be happening, but it did not explain why it was happening to me. For an answer to that I turned to Thoreau directly but I received no response, at least not initially, and I was left to conclude what seemed to me to be the most obvious answer. Thoreau had chosen to speak through me because of the connection I had with Brad, and subsequently, the bond that Brad had with Thoreau, which was built over a lifetime of devotion to his work culminating with the editing and publication of Thoreau's unfinished manuscripts. I thought of myself as a secondary player in this collaboration, selected because of my psychic abilities, my familiarity with Thoreau, my proximity to Concord, and the ease with which I could handle a computer keyboard with my eyes closed. I thought of myself as a psychic transcriptionist and at first I was content to accept that as my role.

Then one day in the spring of 2007 I got to thinking about a psychic reading I'd had soon after I moved to the Boston area in 1984. It had taken place in the back yard of a small house in Lincoln, Massachusetts, near Walden Pond and in an area rightly described as Walden Woods. I had met the psychic when I had signed up for the Past Life Regression class he was teaching one Saturday at The Cambridge Center for Adult Education. He had recently moved to Massachusetts from California, appeared to be in his mid-30s and I remember more now about the way he looked that day, with his long blonde hair and west coast tan, then I remember about any of the past lives that we discussed. At the end of the class, I was excited when he announced that he was giving private readings from his home in Lincoln, and I immediately signed up. A week or so later I was there with him, sitting on folding chairs he had moved into his un-mowed back yard and listening to the words he spoke over the sounds of the nature that surrounded us and the hum of the tape recorder he used to record the session.

In the spring of 2007, after remembering that reading, I knew I needed to find that tape. Over the years I have had many readings that were taped and I never throw things like that out so I knew I still had it stored away in one of the boxes or file cabinets in my office closet, and sure enough, it took me only a few minutes to find it there. As I played it back for the first time in what I would guess at that point was about 20 years, my memories of the event returned to me. The psychic had focused on my present life at first, then began describing the past life images he saw that all felt too distant and remote for me to begin to relate to. Then, as the wind rustled the leaves on the trees that surrounded us, he began to talk about the spirits who he said were there with us in his back yard near Walden Pond.

I was fresh out of Michigan at that time and finally away from that job I'd had there for the prior four years working for the oncologist in Lansing where I had been witness to the slow demise of hundreds of patients, so when that psychic began to talk about the spirits that were there around me I immediately thought of them. I believed the spirits of some of those patients had followed me from Michigan to Massachusetts and the thought that they wanted something more from me than I had already given them made me simply turn away. I didn't want to hear, nor did I hear at the time when that psychic told me that there were spirits there in Lincoln, near Walden Pond, who were circling around me, and one in particular, who was eagerly expressing his desire to work with me, I simply dismissed it. I simply didn't understand. I left that reading, tape in hand, and maybe played it back once or twice during that following year and then I stored it away. The first inkling of what was to be a major part of my life was there in that 60 minute session in 1984 and yet for over 20 years it had been stored away and forgotten. After listening to that tape again in 2007, I finally understood the message it contained and I believe now that it was Thoreau who was there that day in 1984 attempting to connect with me and to set in motion this plan for a collaboration that he, Brad and I had agreed to long ago.

I have always had an interest in Thoreau, and have had many experiences that involved him over the years. I now see how they foreshadowed this event for me. Once during a reading I had with George at Angelica of the Angels in Salem sometime in the late 1990s, George suddenly asked me who that guy was who lived at the pond in Concord. When I said the name "Thoreau" George and I both felt the rush of energy that came into the room, and George observed and I actually felt Thoreau's energy move right through me. George exclaimed, *"Did you feel that?!"* and I acknowledged that I had felt it but later, when discussing the incident with a friend, I had dismissed it as being too incredible to be believed. That is what I always did back then when things like that occurred.

Years later, in the fall of 2005, three months before Brad's sudden passing, I went to see another psychic recommended by a friend, this one in Attleboro, Massachusetts, quite a long drive from Cambridge. This woman had set up her reading space in a small room of an old house right on one of the main streets in town. There was new age music playing throughout our session, used to drown out the sounds of the traffic just outside the window, and it was a long session, involving an energy healing, the first one I had ever had. The best word I can use to describe the state I was left in by it was "elevated" and I suspect it all took place to begin to prepare me for the events that were to transpire during the following year.

Our conversation that day was also preparation. As the psychic worked to free me from the energetic ties I still had then to the dark haired man from my past who I had written about in *Honor in Concord*, we talked about the way I had always felt drawn to Concord and in particular to Thoreau. She acknowledged that there was in fact a bond there and speculated on what my bond with Thoreau might be, focusing primarily on the possibility of a past life together. The conversation then shifted as she described another man who she said would soon be coming into my life. She described him as bright, articulate, and handsome, and said he was successful in his career, and that he would work with me to help me with my writing.

There it was, laid out for me three months before Brad had appeared in my dining room in Cambridge, but at the time it never occurred to me that she might be talking about him. I was certain that other than those brief and awkward encounters I kept having with him at the Thoreau Society gatherings, Brad never gave me a second thought. As the psychic continued she remarked that she was sensing "granite" around this man - which made no sense to either of us at the time and we both laughed at first when I suggested it might have something to do with a cemetery since I would often go up to Author's Ridge in Sleepy Hollow Cemetery in Concord in those days - where the bodies of the Thoreaus, Alcotts, Emersons, and Hawthorne had been buried. She tuned in briefly to consult with her guides and seemed as surprised as I was when it came back to her confirmed. I believe now that the granite she sensed was either a symbol for the afterlife or a reference to New Hampshire's granite, the state where Brad and his wife had been living prior to their move to Indiana. Whatever the case, three months later her prediction came true when this bright, articulate and handsome man came into my life just as she had said he would, but unfortunately it wasn't until after he had passed into spirit.

It is often asked whether the events in our lives are destined to occur or whether we have free will. It seems clear to me that in this case all of the events in my life that led me to Concord, to Thoreau and to Brad were destined to occur, but in 1984, at the time of the reading in Lincoln, I was nowhere near ready to handle something like this. I was still young, immature, unevolved in many respects and had many rows to hoe before I would come to this one. Still, I can't help but wonder had I been more attuned, had I been more open, receptive and willing to listen and not so blindly determined to go my own way, if this experience would have happened sooner and whether it could have happened while Brad was still alive. It seems most likely though, given the prediction made by the psychic in Attleboro that this man would come into my life soon after the first of the year, the exact time when Brad passed into spirit, that this experience was meant to occur at that time and in just this way.

Whatever the case, this episode in my life has convinced me that we do live on after the death of the body, not as some faint, intangible, ethereal creature, but as substantially, willfully, strongly and determinedly as we ever were, and as difficult as it was for me in the beginning as I struggled to understand what was happening, this extraordinary collaboration with Brad and Henry filled my life with purpose, direction, constant inspiration, and love. I was suddenly surrounded by so much love. The uncertainty I had always felt about my own psychic abilities gradually changed as I grew more confident in my perceptions and more ready to speak my own truth at the same time I was speaking theirs. This was a remarkable time for me, inspirational, evolutional, brilliant.

Chapter Five
Walden ~ The Great Adventure

"There is life, our ideas of life, and then there is the life we live."

Henry David Thoreau moved into his cabin at Walden Pond in Concord, Massachusetts on July 4, 1845 and the book he later wrote about his time there entitled, *Walden: Or Life in the Woods (1854)*, is what he is most remembered for. He lived there at Walden until September 6, 1847, and while there he endeavored to do exactly what he states in the second chapter of *Walden*:

> "I went to the woods because I wished to live deliberately, to front only the essential facts of life, and see if I could not learn what it had to teach, and not, when I came to die, discover that I had not lived."

And did he succeed? In the conclusion chapter of *Walden* he states:

> "I learned this, at least, by my experiment: that if one advances confidently in the direction of his dreams, and endeavors to live the life which he has imagined, he will meet with a success unexpected in common hours. He will put some things behind, will pass an invisible boundary; new, universal, and more liberal laws will begin to establish themselves around and within him; or the old laws be expanded, and interpreted in his favor in a more liberal

sense, and he will live with the license of a higher order of beings. "

* * *

After the first transmission, when the words from Thoreau began again he was most interested in talking about his experiences at Walden Pond. This was a topic he returned to many times throughout the channeling and I have chosen to gather most of those transmissions together here in this chapter. I have done the same with other transmissions that shared similar content in the chapters that follow. It is a method of organization that I chose early on as I sorted through the hundreds of pages of transmissions I had received and had to come up with a logical way to present them. I begin with this chapter on Walden because I expect it is an area of most interest for many readers, as it was for me, and also because I am so fond of the following passage where he speaks to me directly (as he does many times throughout the transmissions) and references an expression I often used at the time. Many of my female friends are offended when they hear me use it, but it is never meant by me to be a disparaging remark and in this context it was simply my way of expressing modesty at finding myself involved in a phenomenon such as this with the likes of Thoreau. I knew what was happening was a very big deal and it was hard for me to believe that I was such an integral part of it.

WALDEN: THE GREAT ADVENTURE!

You have an expression, I am just a girl. As I approach Walden I will say, I am just a boy, or was a boy then, still in heart and mind; idealistic in my desire to prove something, or to live in the context of an ideal in my mind. There is life, our ideas of life, and then there is the life we live. I am aware and was aware at the time that there was a difference between who I was and my life as it was when I lived at Walden, and the life that I, through the use of techniques and strategies, organization and artistry, presented in that book. I am me, a man, living in my time, with my associations, my own hurts and desires, insecurities and weaknesses, along with personal strengths. I am a writer, was a writer, as you are the same. We write. We mythologize ourselves and our lives. In a way it was that, but then at some level it was not because the mean life is always more brutal and honest than the recorded version can be. This we know, as writers we know, there is me and the me that I write about and those are two different things.

Those readers who read my work and idealize an image of the man I was fall prey to the inevitable, they believe the image I create is the true image. At best it is my own truest account of myself, but it is not nor will it ever be the truth. For a picture of that more complex structure you must look to other sources, and then there are the pitfalls that come from those sources, because people don't write the truth, so necessarily, they write with their own personal biases. Those who loved and cared for me write with a high bias, a love and light in their hearts, and fond memories of me, the Henry they knew. Those who misunderstood or distrusted or who I gave cause for their ire have written about me less favorably, reflecting their own biases toward negative feelings. They have full right to feel as they do. No doubt I have given them reason for such hostile remembrance, so I accept that as well as a part of myself, knowing full well that none, not my own and not others opinions, whether favorable or not, are a true reflection of me. They are all impressionistic attempts to capture the uncaptureable, for the sincerest essence of who we are at base, our truest and most real selves, are too grand as to be grasped and taken by words, too grand to be masked in praise or rebuke. That essence can be felt and known, but not described.

So in this way I can discuss my experience at Walden. My intentions were pure, my idealism intact and my desire to truly feel and experience something was sincere. I was still a boy in so many ways, striking out on my own at last at age 28. But not on my own as it was borrowed land and often borrowed tools, still it was my own effort and my intention was pure.

Walden Pond was beautiful then, as it remains today. I lived there with squatter's rights on this land that belonged to Waldo[18], and I recorded the events and experiences, more or less, as they occurred and later worked and reworked them into the book that is so well known. Is it then a true account of my time there? Yes, true to whatever extent there can be a true record, but alas, again, there was life at Walden, and then there was the idealized life as it is read and believed.

The purest tranquility is what I felt at Walden. It was for me a place that I could go to for simple privacy, to allow myself the silence I needed to find that place within. It was not that it was so far from society, but any distance is far enough if you have established a private area about yourself, where you can withdraw and reexamine yourself, and that is what I did there.

The level of solitude that I was able to achieve at the pond allowed me to reach a deeper level of myself. I am not sure how much I was aware of when I first went there in terms of what I would find or what my true goal or destiny was. I know that I needed to find a place to live that was not my father's house and was not my friend's house. I needed to have a space of my own and purchasing a farm, as I had once considered, was not the solution for me as I had no intention of ever living a life as most men. So I came up with this idea, as I had heard of other men doing, as Ellery himself had done[19], of taking up life in a small cabin, just enough to suit my needs and pitch it there on the side of the pond. It was as simple as that. We were young and idealistic and that is what we considered a daring and bold move as we were philosophers, intent upon our minds and on a life of contemplation.

---

[18] The land where Thoreau built his cabin at Walden Pond was owned by Ralph Waldo Emerson

[19] Ellery Channing had lived for a time in a hut he built himself in Woodstock, Illinois in 1839.

It was much the opposite from those who strove for communal living, such as that lived at Brook Farm[20] or at Fruitlands[21]. How different my own philosophy was from theirs. I had no desire to join their experiment of communal living, I wanted to find myself not others, and I wanted to do that alone.

ELLERY CHANNING

My friend, Ellery, said that I should go to the pond to devour myself. He understood that need for inner reflection and as his life progressed wished he had more time for it. Ellery and I were kindred souls in a sense, both longing for that connection to a deeper part of ourselves and I was reluctant to give up the sovereignty over my own life that Ellery gave up when he fell in love with his Ellen[22].

Ellery Channing was my friend, a dear friend, kindred in spirit we were, as we sought out a deeper experience of life than what others might have. His remark to me about devouring myself at the pond seemed ironic to me later, as I felt that the children and the wife that he tied himself to had devoured him, or at least attempted to. He resisted their frenzied need of him for most of his life, resenting the costs and the demands that they placed on him. Ellery envied the freedom I had, but then of myself, was I so free?

---

[20] A communal living community formed in Jamaica Plains, MA in 1841 by transcendentalist and Unitarian Minister, George Ripley (1802-1880). Among the inhabitants of Brook Farm were Nathaniel Hawthorne and Margaret Fuller. Thoreau visited but did not join.

[21] A utopian community formed at Harvard, Massachusetts by Amos Bronson Alcott (1799-1888) and his friend, Englishman, Charles Lane (1800-1870), who was one of the founders of Alcott House, a progressive school in Surrey, England devoted to Alcott's principles of education and named for him. Many who lived at Brook Farm, joined Alcott and Lane at Fruitlands. Author, Louisa May Alcott, was a child when her father moved the family to Fruitlands.

[22] Ellery Channing married Ellen Fuller, sister of transcendentalist writer, Margaret Fuller, on September 23, 1841. They had five children together, but Ellery was unable to handle the responsibilities of being husband and father. He was frequently absent and Ellen cited abuse as her reason for leaving the marriage in 1853. After her death in 1856, the children were left to be raised by other family members and Ellery was estranged from them for the rest of his life.

My ties to my family would never be broken, but when the need is lacking in one for emotional ties beyond his family, or for sexual intimacy when one is so inept and ill prepared for that venture, and he seeks instead and finds something else to fulfill him, then it is not for him a lonely or a sorrowful life because he does lead the life best suited for him.

THE SOLITUDE

There were times when the solitude I craved at Walden was available to me and I basked in it. I would on sunny days position myself there in my doorway and allow myself to sink as deeply as I could into the surrounding atmosphere, into the waves of light and energy that flowed to me and drift as far as I could out into that universe and let myself sense myself as that free and noble creature that I knew existed within me. Those were times that I fully understood that I was more than this body that I had come to occupy. This I understood without question, for I could lift my hand and view it and know that it was not my hand and these were not my feet, and this was but a vehicle with which I drove. I learned to settle myself, my mind and my breath, into a relaxed posture and enjoyed those moments of sheer reverie in the universe. Traveling that way was cheaper in fact than travel any other way, and the rewards were great. Each time I ventured out I felt this greater spirit within me. Each time knowing more and more confidently that there was something beyond, something more to this life than the material acquisitions.

OCCUPATION

I did not have an occupation while at the pond, other than the time I spent writing in my journal, and other than the time spent tending to the crops I grew. I learned much in those days of hoeing that field, much by way of monitoring the seasons, the way the rain would fall to feed and enrich the soil that would later house the seeds that would grow to the beans that would feed me. This life sustaining process was in itself a fascination for me. This is how the system works that provides the food that we need to sustain life. I look upon all nature as a system that works in harmony. That harmony is not something that I see in human interactions.

INTELLECT

There ceases to be harmony in human interactions because of the presence of the intellect. Does a coyote spend time thinking and rethinking his choice to kill in order to eat? No, it is his nature to seek his prey and kill his prey in order to consume it in order to sustain his own life. It is the presence of the intellect that prevents harmony in man's own interaction. His propensity to thought, to think through his actions, and his awareness of himself and his actions, prevents him from ever being in harmony with it. That is the difficulty.

THE ANIMALS

At Walden, on a clear crisp morning, the sun is reflecting off the pond. I am there, surveying the shoreline, taking it in. It is special the way the day dawns at the pond, so different than it looks in town with the mass of dust all the time, the sounds and the smells of horses - kept - and cows, barnyard animals, captive animals. I wonder at why there is such smell from the captive animals and in nature the smells combine in a more sensually pleasing way. This is just something that crosses my mind. I look at the horses sometimes and see they are slaves, much as the people who are enslaved, held in bondage. The animals are held in the same way. Here at the pond and in the woods that surround, the animals are free, free to experience their lives, free to master their own destinies.

It is said by some that I could speak to the animals at the pond. Speaking is a mechanism for conveying information through sound, but with the animals it is different for they don't recognize the sounds or process those sounds as words and understand their meaning, but they do understand and sense my intent as I speak to them, so in that sense, yes I spoke to them. Beyond that, it was a matter of trust. After a period of time that I lived at the pond, after they observed my manner of living, where I acted in ways to preserve life there, not to take it, and tried to work within the simple ethos of their society, then they learned to trust. It did not hurt that I often offered them food to help to coax them, or that through repetition they learned certain actions and routine. It was not unlike a circus performer who trains their captive animals to behave in certain ways, except in my case the animals were not my slaves, they were my neighbors, and there was no act of domination on my part to get them to perform. They simply acted and reacted to me as they would, judging me a peaceful and non-threatening presence. They went about their day just as I went about mine. The most important factor in this discourse between myself and these creatures was that I recognized them as a critical part of the life force on this planet and a part that should not be taken advantage of or caused to suffer needlessly in any way. They are sentient and sensate beings, aware of the life around them, and an integral part of it. I recognized within them the same divinity that was present within me.

VEGETARIANISM

As I discuss animals, I must discuss the issue of vegetarianism that has often been associated with those like me who consider themselves transcendentalists. Bronson Alcott[23] was the truest transcendentalist in that sense, the truest to his truest principles, as he could rise to the level of fanaticism in his devotion to things. For myself, I believed in the sacred nature of all life, and sought not to take life and did consume far less flesh than most average men in my time, but I was not a pure vegetarian and there were occasions when I would eat meat.

I was always conscious of the source of what I consumed and continued to believe that a clean diet would not include the intake

---

[23] Amos Bronson Alcott (1799-1882) innovative educator and transcendentalist, father of author, Louisa May Alcott.

of flesh. However, I understood that flesh eating was part of nature. The animals themselves subsisted by consuming each other for food. As harsh as that reality is, it is the way of nature. It is a predatory system designed to support itself and every part of nature is in some way consumed. That is reality as it was and continues to be. Yet, there are today and there were in my time, meat production factories that exist for the purpose of slaughtering animals for food. That manner of raising animals in captivity for the purpose of destroying them is a level of cruelty toward animals that must stop. We cannot continue to treat our fellow occupants on this planet with such cruelty. Man has a source of good within, but too he has cruelty and what some might call evil. It is all there, as it is all there within the universe, so it is reflected in man.

THE HOUSE AT WALDEN

Entering into the house at Walden I was free at last, in many ways, as I looked about that small space and knew the most basic of my needs were met. I had shelter, I had food, I had warmth, I had enough clothes, and I had a "root cellar" to protect my food from the rain. Listen to me for what I had there was freedom. I did not have my mind all day impacted by the thoughts of others or by images of the world displayed on a television screen before me and causing me disharmony. I had peace, and within that peace and quiet I could then control the ebb and flow of my own thoughts. I could record my own visions, and I could seek to understand that which I did not understand. I sought many answers through the nature that surrounded me and I learned that there is a truth within nature that is unlike any other you will ever see. I was never lied to by a mouse or a wood chuck. I was never deceived by a beautiful bird. I drifted in my canoe on the pristine waters and looked into the heavens at night full of stars and understood the depth and the breadth of this place that I was inhabiting, and the depth and breadth of the space that was within me. I saw it all and it was sublime.

"Both place and time were changed, and I dwelt nearer to those parts of the universe and to those eras in history which had most attracted me."
- Henry David Thoreau, Walden (1854)

LIFE AT WALDEN

And so I began to understand and to gain my own thoughts and position on life while living at Walden. In that respect I succeeded in sucking out the marrow of life, because I reached its deepest understanding. Then later I constructed the book, in the hopes of conveying that message. To start with the practical matters, this is how I built my house. This is the amount of energy and time and expense that went into it and this is what I had. I had the bare essentials of life, why should I or anyone else need more? I listed it out, my cot, my desk, my chair, my extra chairs, for company and for society. I had my wood stove, to warm my home in foul weather, and the broom I needed to keep my home clean. I had little in the knickknack variety because if there was no other purpose for an item but for decoration in my home, then I could soon do without it. Nature around me was all the decoration that I needed to see.

After creating for myself a proper structure to protect myself from the elements, then I set out to describe my methods for collecting a living, methods that would not overly tax my body or my time, and that would provide enough food to sustain me. I have already admitted that there were times when my diet was supplemented through the kindness of family and friends. I do not see this as a contradiction, as the majority of my time I provided my own food from my own efforts at the pond. My goal was to outline a manner in which all men could live simpler lives, with less labor and less time taken from their lives. To me this was a grander style of living than that lived by any other man who worked all the time in his day in order to afford a larger and nicer home. No man should be judged worthwhile simply by the total of his possessions, but should be judged by what lies within him. The richness of who we are lies within.

That was my philosophy, and however extreme it may be seen by some, I truly believed in the ideal, whether or not I fully lived up to it. Yet this is a flaw that many see in my character. Even this author is skeptical of the motives behind what I do. She herself suffers from a certain degree of social discomfort, and she sees this in me and believes it is the motivation behind my lack of ambition. There could be some truth in that, as I have previously said. It did suit me well to take this course, and to speak to these beliefs that life can be better if lived more simply. But perhaps I am made in the way that I was made and she is made as she so that we are best suited to carry the messages we bring. Had she a child or grandchild to attend to today, I doubt she would be sitting here connecting to and tending to me. We are made as we are sometimes to better suit our own missions.

At the time that I lived at Walden the simple living that I longed for and later wrote about was threatened by the influx of technology and people. We were no longer a distant knoll of a town in Concord, we were now accessible by train and that meant more people, more ideas, and more activities. The pace of the town changed as the outside world ushered in. These were difficult times for me to endure as I could see a slipping away from a simpler experience of life. We were losing our connection to nature and spirit and connecting instead to materialistic needs and desires, equating the worth of self to value of our material possessions.

At Walden I could hear the train horn blow as it approached or departed Concord, knowing it would soon pass by and I waited for it and wondered at the way it distracted me from all things of value. Even the birds and the animals were disrupted from their daily course. What was life now to them with this sound running through the area that had never been heard before? How did it change their lives to wonder now at this new thing for life was not as it was and would never be again.

WRITING WALDEN

It is an artistic endeavor to put together a book such as *Walden*, and that is what I engaged in for years after I left the pond, writing and rewriting, adding and subtracting, shaping and forming it into a workable piece. It is my most remembered book because of the message it conveys, but also for the stories and the images it contains.

There were many books that I guess I could have written, if I wanted. My brother, John would more have preferred a mystery story or some exciting adventure be told. I thought of that often, as I wrote *Walden*. He would have preferred a more adventurous book, not the serious solemnity of *Walden*, but I did weave into the book as many humorous passages as I could.

You do not ever get over those who you love who have passed before you and at times I did feel my brother was there with me. I would speak to him and would sometimes sense his reply, so it was not without company that I lived at the pond. He was another of the guests that I had there. It left me in a state of longing, but also understanding, knowing that one day I would see him again, and that I did.

A WEEK ON THE CONCORD AND MERRIMACK RIVERS

The book that I wrote at Walden I put together from journal entries I made while on a boating trip with my brother. What became clear to me on that journey was that the river that flows so slowly and peacefully through my home town was at its base an enormously different thing. It is a vast world, so many different places and people and yet all tied together by the bodies of water that flow through. At the ocean's shore you can set your bare foot into the water and sense that vastness. I never looked at the rivers in Concord the same way again after that trip, and I loved more the simple purity of Walden, and the fact that the source of its water was hidden somehow and it was there isolated and pure and pristine. It became more significant to me then as a place to find peace.

A P E R F E C T P L A C E

The time I spent at Walden influenced my life for the rest of my life. Walden was for me a perfect place, a refuge, an escape, a place where I could truly be me and do as I pleased without the constant refrain from neighbors, he will amount to nothing. I will amount to more than nothing, but they will have their opinions, and I will have my own.

M O O N L I G H T W A L K A T W A L D E N

In the north sky there is a moon this night, as he walks alone along the trail. There are no street lights to light his path, he does not carry any illumination, yet he follows the path slowly and deliberately and, with the aid of the moon, he finds his way back to his home at the pond.

Inside, he builds a fire and lights a candle and the warmth in the small space cradles around him. He is alone and yet wanting for no one and nothing. He is perfect, relaxed, warmed and comfortable. This for him is total satisfaction. This fulfills him as he drifts into sleep.

THE MESSAGE

Chapter Six
Channeling

"We are enormous, each of us, and so profoundly important..."

When the channeling began I had no idea how long it would last or how many transmissions there would be but soon it was like the flood gates had opened. Any time I would sit down at my computer, poised and ready and focus, even for a second, the flow of words would resume and I continued to record them as they came to me. The pace of the transmissions would usually be timed to match the pace of my transcription, but there were times when they would tease me to see whether or not I could keep up if the speed of the transmissions increased. More than once Thoreau remarked about how fast I was able to transcribe his words. There were aspects of this modern world that he seemed to be genuinely intrigued by.

There were days when I wasn't interested in sitting at the computer with eyes closed and my hands on the keyboard that I would be prompted to return there, but it was always my choice and most times I would comply. On the days when I had an issue in mind that I wanted to talk about, the words I received would often address that issue. Other days, when I was distracted by things going on in my life, I would receive wise counsel from Thoreau himself. I have removed most of those type of remarks from the manuscript because they seem to me to be simply too private and not relevant to the purpose of this book. I mention them only as a way to describe how relaxed and comfortable this process was. There was nothing domineering about it, nothing negative or disruptive. There was just a calm resolve, I believe on all our parts, along with a determination that grew over time, that we were going to put this book together the best way we could. This book was never intended to be, nor is it, a scholarly assessment of Thoreau's work, as even now, he continues to scoff at things considered academic or scholarly. His intent for this book, as I understand it, was to call our attention back to the fundamental truths that have always been there in the words he left behind.

I was not always aware of the meaning in the transmissions I received as I typed them. I suppose it would have distracted me if I had been. It was always later when I went back over the material, when I was removing the typos or misspellings that were the result of my own typing speed or lack of grammatical skills, that I found the meaning there so plain to see. It was in those moments, perhaps more than any others, that I became convinced that the words that I was receiving were not originating with me. There was too much information coming through that was new to me. There were thoughts and observations that I had never had before and references made to materials I had never read before. As I previously stated, up until this time I had been a passionate researcher into the lives of the Concord writers, a literary historian of sorts, but I wasn't in any way a scholar of Thoreau's work. Even though I had been a member of the Thoreau Society for several years, I had never completely read *Walden* or any of Thoreau's essays, other than the vain attempts I had made at reading them in high school and college. I was a student of Thoreau when this process began but that changed though as time went on, when I found myself suddenly possessing information about Thoreau and his work that I had not come upon in any conventional way. I was receiving downloads of information. I would wake up some mornings more knowledgeable about Thoreau and his work than I had been the night before, and I would find myself responding to things written or said about him in the media, even by other Thoreauvians, that I knew were wrong and that I knew he disputed. It was inexplicable and sometimes confusing, but overall this collaboration that I was engaged in with Thoreau and Brad was exhilarating.

There was a disagreement between us, however, when it came to my idea about how to present this material versus theirs. They would have preferred that I write a more conventional book, one that presented their ideas as if they were in fact my own, but I refused to do that. I wanted to share the experience along with the message, because to me the revelation that we do live on after our physical deaths and that it is in fact possible to communicate with those in spirit, is as important as any other message this book might contain. I believe that revelation changes everything.

* * *

The following journal entry dated August 1838 was written by Thoreau when he was only 21 years old. It is my favorite of all of the words he wrote during his lifetime because it demonstrates his awareness of consciousness even at that young age. The sensation of floating and being at one with the universe that he describes was critical for me in allowing the channeling to take place. It was while "gamboling familiarly" through my own depths that I was able to connect not just to Thoreau's consciousness but to my own.

If with closed ears and eyes I consult consciousness for a moment – immediately are all walls and barriers dissipated – earth rolls from under me, and I float, by the impetus derived from the earth and the system – a subjective – heavily laden thought, in the midst of an unknown & infinite sea, or else heave and swell like a vast ocean of thought – without rock or headland. Where are all riddles solved, all straight lines making there their two ends to meet – eternity and space gamboling familiarly through my depths. I am from the beginning – knowing no end, no aim. No sun illumines me, – for I dissolve all lesser lights in my own intenser and steadier light - I am a restful kernel in the magazine of the universe. - Henry David Thoreau, Journal, August 1838

Thoreau had this to say about consciousness.

C O N S C I O U S N E S S

It is the idea of reaching other levels of existence through silent meditation that underscores the process of my life. I found a way to travel within the sphere of my own mind and spirit, and that avenue is there and readily available to anyone who chooses it. I found the deepest satisfaction in my life through this inner travel.

I am at heart a seeker, an explorer into the true nature of life. If you want to know me better, and if you want to see who I really am, then you must understand that as an elemental part of my existence. There was in me this desire to explore, to know and to understand the truth about life that was present from an early age. I simply knew that there had to be something more to this life than the physical ramifications of society.

I found truth first in the workings of nature. It was a perfect, flawless system. Seeds begat flowers, begat seeds, begat flowers. The wind spread the seeds that grew to flowers. It was all a hodgepodge of bright colors and designs and life, joyful and rugged, and it all worked together to create perfect form and perfect beauty, and how, just how could this be? What was it that drove it? That's what I asked, that's what I most wanted to know, and what I came to believe was that the force that was there within nature was also there within me.

S O L I T U D E

"Ah! I need solitude. I have come forth to this hill at sunset to see the forms of the mountains in the horizon - to behold and commune with something grander than man. Their mere distance and unprofanedness is an infinite encouragement. it is with infinite yearning and aspiration that I seek solitude, more and more resolved and strong; but with a certain weakness that I seek society ever."
- Henry David Thoreau, Journal, August 14, 1854

We are never alone because we are a part of the larger system of spirit that is in place here. An individual life is but one act in a long play of the spirit. I was aware of this at the time I wrote *Walden* when I referred to the doubleness of our natures. There is me and also this separate awareness of me that is always looking down and in some ways judging the other. Some would call that double me the higher self that is keeping tabs on the lower one. The lower self is the one who is here to act in the play. The higher self is ever present, watching and choreographing our every move. In that sense then there is never solitude, because we are always connected to our own higher selves and to the larger system of spirit as well.

Of course there is a type of solitude that can be achieved when we limit our communication with or interference from others. In our interactions with others all of our thoughts, even those we don't express, are shared in some way, and all of our actions have an impact, too, whether for good or for bad. It is a mutual exchange for the purpose of learning, but there is often a taxing quality to our interactions that cause many, and it certainly caused me, to want to retreat.

The greatest gift I gave myself at Walden was this type of solitude. I created a distance and space around myself where I could focus on myself and not be disrupted by the concerns or the demands of others. The knowledge that I gained through this experience has had a great impact on many so you see our solitary time is as valuable as that which we spend with others.

We should encourage those who seek to gain knowledge or to excel in any way for we are each benefited by each other's successes and we are each deterred by each other's failures. That is simple fact and law.

We are enormous, each of us, and so profoundly important in ways that we have never imagined. This I can assure you, your concerns, even the pettiest of them, amount to far more than a "hill of beans" in this universe.

* * *

With that we were out of time for the day but rather than quickly break the connection, as I most often did, I hesitated. I could sense that there was something more that Thoreau wanted to say.

We can draw to a close now. It has been a productive afternoon. We will soon have a book to show for our commitment and perseverance, but there is much more to come, as we are only beginning. I will be here waiting when you return, seated here on this fallen tree at Walden. In the remotest part of your mind you will find your connection to me.

Chapter Seven
The Beauty in Life and Nature

"Nature is a perfect system. Man's system of living is not."

*"We get only transient and partial glimpses of the beauty of the world.
Standing at the right angle, we are dazzled by the colors of the rainbow
in colorless ice. From the right point of view, every storm and every drop
in it is a rainbow. Beauty and music are not mere traits and exceptions.
They are the rule and character. It is the exception that we see and
hear." - Henry David Thoreau, Journal, December 11, 1855*

When we connected again and the transmissions resumed the
following morning it seemed as if Thoreau had been there all the
while I was away patiently awaiting my return, but then time as we
know it does not exist in the world of spirit. Even if he did stay there
at Walden waiting for me as he had said that he would, I expect that
for him it was as if I had never left at all.

THE BEAUTY IN LIFE
AND NATURE

You are back, indeed, and stronger I see. What have I been
thinking of as I waited here on this tree? The beauty of life - that is
what I thought of - that there is such beauty in life and beauty in
nature and so much of that ignored.

I am known for my love of nature and my desire to preserve it.
Yes, do go out and fight to preserve nature! Do not let it be
overrun by your industries! Do not let the land that is home to the
animals be overtaken and destroyed! Please, do use my image to

defend nature in this way! I stand proudly behind any endeavor that sets out to preserve nature, and if nothing more is taken from my work than that, then I am satisfied, but of course there is more.

What I saw in nature was perfect harmony. It was as if the greatest art, the greatest music, the greatest written words were all there within this thing called nature, but nothing that man produced could be as grand as what God had produced. To watch a seed grow to flower, and that flower to later produce a seed. That was glory to me to see that complex and yet simple process unfold.

Yet, when I saw that same process unfold in man, a child being born, growing to adult and producing more children, I did not view that so beautifully. It seemed nature was always renewing itself and in nature it was adding more to what I saw as a perfect system. When I saw another child born I saw it more as another tax on the earth. As long as man is not in harmony with the earth, then all men and the products of men will not be in harmony with the earth.

> *"I do not know where to find in any literature, whether ancient or modern, any adequate account of that Nature with which I am acquainted" - Henry David Thoreau, Journal, February 1851*

DISHARMONY IN MAN

> *"Of course it is of no use to direct our steps to the woods, if they do not carry us thither. I am alarmed when it happens that I have walked a mile into the woods bodily, without getting there in spirit.... What business have I in the woods, if I am thinking of something out of the woods?" -Henry David Thoreau, Walking (1851)*

Nature is a perfect system. Man's system of living is not. There is no pretense or speculation in nature. Each element of nature is what it is. The fish in the stream swim because they are fish. They do not arise each day and wonder am I a fish or a frog? Nature makes it clear to them and they follow that course. If man could be as perfect within his own nature, then there would be less strife in the world.

When I am in the woods I am as much a part of nature as the deer is a part of nature, but many men go into the woods and are unaffected by it. It is as if they are from a foreign land and the deer see them as such and fear them. The deer never feared me.

In summer here there are the many beachgoers who come to the pond to frolic and play in the water, to bake in the sun and to soil and abuse the land and disregard all right of animal or sensate soul to pass through. Many do not have a highly developed sense of their own spirituality, so what do they get for their time in nature? They get dust on their new white sneakers or a poison ivy rash on their leg. They ski on its mountains, hike in its woods, and return home, perhaps for a short time enriched by their experience, but soon they return to their ordinary pursuits, for greater achievement at work, for material goods, the things for which they value themselves and their lives.

Others, like me, who are aware of the spiritual presence within them, are enriched and motivated and reaffirmed by nature in ways that no church or preacher or even poet could provide for them. Theirs is the truest and healthiest experience of nature. Nature reflects back to us the very nature of ourselves and the nature of ourselves and all things is spirit.

We must learn to live in harmony with nature just as the animals do. Only then will we be truly human, not divided by religion or race or sect, but united by our common humanity and our common spirituality. Then and only then will we find peace.

"The more thrilling, wonderful, divine objects I behold in a day, the more expanded and immortal I become."
- Henry David Thoreau, Wild Fruits (2001)

"The beauty of the earth answers exactly to your demand and appreciation." - Henry David Thoreau, Journal, November 2, 1858

THE DEADLY HUM

"The other evening I was determined that I would silence this shallow din; that I would walk in various directions and see if there was not to be found any depth of silence around." - Thoreau, Letter to H.B.O. Blake, August 8, 1854

As a child I ran through the fields of Concord un-abetted by the constant stream of information that runs now through this time. It is like a deadly hum to me, this constant noise that permeates all things and pollutes. They worry about the pollution of the atmosphere, the global warming, the environmental pollution, and yet they continue to promote pollution in the media. There it is anything goes, so those items that are the equivalent of poison are displayed with the same measure of consideration as those which are worthwhile, healthful and nurturing for the body and soul. All are there within the hum.

That which pollutes the mind and body is as bad as that which pollutes the rivers and streams. Do you not see that? Do you not understand that you have exposed your mind and your body to pollution? For we also see it in the food that is produced. What is this thing in this box that can still be fresh six months from now, or in this can that can be eaten two years from now? I suspect what it contains cannot be fresh or food of any kind and that it cannot hold much nutrition if it can be held that long for by then any nutrients it might contain are surely dead.

That which passes for food is poison. That which passes for art or entertainment or news is poison. Where is the truth in it? Why are you no longer able to see and discern that which is good and bad for you? You give the equivalency to that which is purely wrong to that which is right. It is not so! It is a sign that you have lost your connection to that which is the truest part of you. It is by strengthening your ties to the knowledge within you that you will begin to see and identify truth in all things.

MODERN MARVELS

"A man is wise with the wisdom of his time only, and ignorant with its ignorance. Observe how the greatest minds yield in some degree to the superstitions of their age." - Henry David Thoreau, Journal, Jan. 30, 1853

Here it is 150 years after my time and all that I have warned of has come to pass. I do not yet see where it has settled in that you are so much more than you appear to be, it seems now you are so much less. Much has happened to make your lives inferior, not superior, in my estimation. You think the modern marvels have improved your lives, but they have not. Gone is the relationship between nature and yourselves. You are forever clothed and cloaked and held back from the reality of who you are. If you are clean and powdered or perfumed and readied for public appearance, you are very nearly no longer human, and yet this makes you more acceptable to the masses of humankind. You see, if you reflect in any way your animal nature then you are banished and left out from the group.

You must today show your absolute superiority over your circumstances, show that you have the most beautiful hair and clothes, cars and homes, the biggest televisions, the most powerful computers, or God knows what else, in order to show that you are the worthiest of men. I say this makes you the non-worthiest and respect more those who know who they are and reflect upon it in an unhidden way. Why dress in better and better dresses? Why wear jewels that require you to spend your time each day in pursuit of more wealth in order to maintain your haberdashery? That is what I ask, for I see the fault in all of that. I see where the ideal fails to truly satisfy.

THE BODY

You cannot mask the body in finery and expect that it will not then be the same weak, smelly and rugged body that it is, because without a small degree of care it will become this dismissible relic within a short time and it will soon be tossed aside and buried or burned and then what? Then you deal with what you have left. If all you were was that body, then you are lost for you no longer have that body. If all you were was the possessions that body owned, then you are lost for you no longer have those possessions. They are gone to your children or your spouse or your siblings or friends and you stand back as spirit and watch how they mistreat the things you once cherished. It is out of your control and you see then that you are nothing, because when body and possessions are all that you have then once they are gone, you stand alone. And what then do you see? What I saw was me. I saw me, the real me, and I saw the light that shined before me and I knew that I was a part of that light and I wanted to merge with it and be brought back into the land of God and Godlike things which is our true home.

CALAMITY

"We should treat our minds, that is, ourselves, as innocent and ingenuous children, whose guardians we are, and be careful what objects and what subjects we thrust on their attention." - Henry David Thoreau, Life Without Principle (1863)

If I were of life today I would look around at the calamity that has befallen man and ask: *"Where is the value?"* That is what I would want to know. The media has taken hold and now forms the minds of all. Television programs that lack any conscience or morality pour out into the living rooms across the nation. What have we here - political and cultural bankruptcy, demonization of those who are not demons and sainthood for those who are just better than demons? It is as it would never have been if anyone were watching and listening closely enough and knowing with good faith their own truth.

Too much time is spent staring at television and computers in a dull and listless way, passively absorbing whatever useless information is being sprung on you. There is something mesmerizing and hypnotizing in the process and there is little discrimination in the intake of the information that is received. I warn those who watch and listen to do so with a cautious ear, retake your focus and do not allow your minds and your characters to be molded by the wisdomless wisdom that comes to you through that device.

I do not say that there is nothing of value there. Surely such technology would have mesmerized the people of my day as well. If, for instance, a television had played in that small house at Walden, if perhaps a radio was playing, or I had a computer on hand, then I might have indulged in such things for a short while, but I say, as I have said about all things, that we must use our own powers of discrimination to judge the worthiness of the information that is put before us before we take it in.

By putting yourself down in front of a television screen or computer monitor you are leaving yourselves open to the information whether it be good or bad that flows from it. Where is the discernment that is needed to sort through the information that comes to you from that place? Where is that quality of knowing and how can you attain it? That is the biggest question. That is what must be answered, for if you sit in front of such a device and allow your mind to meld into the experience of it and allow yourself to believe what is conveyed to you without question, then you have stepped aside and another is now in control of your mind. That is the fear for you have allowed yourself to lose your own individuality. You have lessened your own freedom.

The experience is one of loss, losing a part of yourself in an effort to entertain yourself, losing what is the purity and function of your wise mind. You must stand firm and steady and protect that which you already have, your tie to truth. You must see it and know it and experience it within you, and once you do there will be little that can sway you.

There is no truth that can be found anywhere that cannot first be found within you. Know that, and understand that.

"We do not live for idle amusement."
- Henry David Thoreau, Life Without Principle (1863)

TRUTH

It has always been the responsibility of the individual to seek out truth for themselves. If you believe something is true simply because it is told to you then you are bound to find that you do not have truth at all. It is through the ability to test and measure the information you receive that is innate within each of us that you will find truth. That is a skill that must be formed and one that can then be relied upon with little effort.

Any and all who seek to find truth will find it. Seek to find wisdom as well. Wise action brings wise results. Slow, bored, inattention brings low results. This can be applied to all aspects of life. Just as there are those who are so completely physically soft and overweight, so there are minds that are the same. The mind must be heightened and in full awareness and it will seek to be so.

Repetitive computer games and low level television programs capture the attention but also serve to deaden the senses and lesson the function and the awareness of the mind. You are not educated by the constant influx of low knowledge or benefited by having extra pounds because of an excess of sweets. Neither does the technology you allow to rule your life lift your self esteem or make you a happier or worthier person. Cartoons do not feed a mind. Candy does not feed a body. These are the principles to be understood. Input equals output. Consume the best and finest in wisdom and you will become wise, consume a diet of sugar and you will become weak. There is no argument against this, is there?

For anyone who reads this and is feeling a depth of despair and unhappiness in their lives, I suggest that you do as I did, minimize your possessions, and more importantly your attachment to them, and focus your thoughts instead on that simple place of silence within you. That is how you will find perfect harmony and balance. That is where you will find your truest self.

Empower yourselves by seeking truth. Return to the purity of your spirits. Make your minds sacred chambers and your bodies the gospel temples that they should be. Then you will have begun to live. Then you will have begun to see.

* * *

"All health and success does me good, however far off and withdrawn it may appear; all disease and failure helps to make me sad and does me evil, however much sympathy it may have with me or I with it."
- Henry David Thoreau, Walden (1854)

"What you call bareness and poverty is to me simplicity."
- Henry David Thoreau, Letter to H.G.O. Blake, December 5, 1856

Chapter Eight
The Universe in You

"The mysterious grows more mysterious at times."

"However intense my experience, I am conscious of the presence and criticism of a part of me, which, as it were, is not a part of me, but spectator, sharing no experience, but taking note of it, and that is no more I than it is you. When the play, it may be the tragedy, of life is over, the spectator goes his way. It was a kind of fiction, a work of the imagination only, so far as he was concerned. This doubleness may easily make us poor neighbors and friends sometimes."
- Henry David Thoreau, Walden (1854)

As the months went by and the transmissions continued I became more aware of that part of me that was, as Thoreau describes, the spectator. To me, that was my higher self, the true me, the sum of all my parts, my totality, and the one who I credit with having agreed to this collaboration with Henry and Brad in the first place. The trouble for me was that I, as puppet, often lacked faith in the I that was my puppet master. So, no matter how consistent and reliable the communications with Thoreau were and no matter how many times I was reassured, both by him during the transmissions, and by the psychics who I sometimes consulted for a "reality check" along the way, I continued to wonder whether what I was experiencing could be considered real at all. Still, it went on, and each day that I sat at my computer connecting with spirit, I allowed myself to venture deeper into their realm. I would become totally focused and completely lost in what I was doing, no longer conscious of time or of my surroundings, and after a while I could no longer hear the incessant and endless sounds of truck engines that emitted from what I called the "dirt farm" that was located on the property behind the townhouse where I lived then in Bedford.

I never understood what it was they were doing at the dirt farm. I knew their business was in some way connected to New England Nurseries, a gardening center that was just a short distance up on Route 62, but every day, as I sat at my desk perfecting my ability to connect to spirit, and learning to trust more fully in the words I was receiving, those trucks were there, pushing, pulling, re-stacking and rearranging their piles of dirt - that most basic element of the physical planet on which we live and rely. Surprisingly, it was in those moments when my focus most intensified, not on the noises and the distractions of this physical world, but on my own consciousness and the consciousness of the universe as well. The louder the trucks became the easier it was for me to connect with spirit and the more the words flowed. There was a sense of drifting in those moments that was truly liberating. It was in those moments that I would let go of the doubt. It was in those moments when I felt gifted and blessed. I knew happenings like this were rare, but I was not dreaming. It was real. I felt alive. I felt free.

WEEDS

You are different in your mood of late. It is hard to pinpoint exactly what caused the change. The mysterious grows more mysterious at times. This is a difficult thing to process, no doubt of that. How you walk through a normal life with this reality is baffling for even me to discover and of course from here we see that it is all quite real and valid. From your perspective it is so much more like a dream, like something that is experienced but is never thought of in real terms, or acknowledged as existing at all, and yet spirit is there, always there, and people are tripping over it, walking into it, walking through it. In your case, gentle you who sometimes warms to it, talking as you lie in bed to the one in spirit. That is a pretty picture to me, a dear exchange and you should view it in that way. Do not question those moments, they are well received, and well experienced in the loving way they are intended. Most of the weeds in your garden if overlooked will simply fade away. There are only weeds as you allow them to grow. I say, grow no more weeds!

It amuses me that you have taken on the challenge presented to you, although at first you fought fiercely against it. I, too, was like you, fighting authority in all forms. You must not ever tell me what to do, I knew what I should do, knew what was best. I suppose in many ways I did know and I support wholeheartedly your right to personal sovereignty of all kinds, up to the point when your sovereignty overtakes mine, but alas those are more difficult topics.

THE INNER MAN

I do not think that any man who lives can deny the levels of emotion within him. We have each felt every emotion be it anger, rage, jealousy, loneliness, compassion, or love. All emotions are expressions of the God force that is at work on this planet. Perhaps the truest expression is the combination of all of these, the mixing of all into a healthy pot.

At the pond I would make stew, some part of this and some part of that, all stirred together to create a delicious brew. It is the blending of the different seasonings that make such a fine stew, and that is a metaphor that should be understood for every aspect of life. It is the mixing of the various cultures and ideas and perspectives on life that make the finest and truest brew.

No one who claims a particular perspective should claim that perspective as the only worthy one. There isn't only one perspective or one path in life. There are many different paths available for many different people. It is up to the individual to find the best path for themselves, and that is what I advocate most. The more variety, the more knowledge, the more experience of the individual, the more we each experience collectively. Each one of us feeds the pot.

"If a man does not keep pace with his companions, perhaps it is because he hears a different drummer. Let him step to the music which he hears, however measured or far away." - Henry David Thoreau, Walden (1854)

PERSONAL FREEDOM

If I stand for nothing else, let me stand and be remembered as a voice that spoke to freedom, freedom for the individual to self determine, and to find within himself his truest nature. That is what most inspires and inspired me.

Society has no right to tell a man how to live, to hinder his personal freedom in any way, so if a man chooses a particular path because of events of his life that have formed him in a certain way, then so be it his choice and his destiny. Let him have the freedom not to conform, but to find instead another way to live, and let him live without judgment. There should be no judgment upon a man who chooses to live life outside society's frame.

There are many like me, and like this author, who find meaning in life by their own design. There is this born within each of us, this ability to construct and design our own lives. This is what lies at the core of true spiritual experience and expression, when we recognize ourselves as part of this greater whole and we learn to view ourselves in co-sponsorship with it.

"As long as possible live free and uncommitted."
- Henry David Thoreau, Walden (1854)

THE SECRET

"I learned this, at least, by my experiment; that if one advances confidently in the direction of his dreams, and endeavors to live the life which he has imagined, he will meet with a success unexpected in common hours." - Henry David Thoreau, Walden (1854)

You do not fully realize, and few do, how powerfully we reign over our own destinies. There is much talk of late in this world of the "secret".[24] To me it is not a secret and never was a secret that our actions have results, that our talk, our thoughts, our desires, our feelings create actual events in our lives. You must learn to master your own power and abilities and then, only then, will you have the life that you want.

Each of our burdens and each of our days' labors are time taken away from the simple enjoyment of life. I do not understand why that simple concept is not more obvious. Perhaps it is and that is why I said and still maintain that the mass of men lead lives of quiet desperation.[25] They feel no contact to the spirit within them and see their life only as a series of tasks and chores, hard work that they despise to bring in sufficient income to feed their families, warm their homes, and support their meager existence. I do not say meager because of the poor quality of the home where they reside, but I say meager because of the poor quality of the attachment that they have to the spirit within them.

It is true that for all people the secret, the only true secret, is the one that resides within, the one that is always there, that secret is this: we are spirit, tied to spirit, equal in this shared divinity. That is the secret. We are magical and miraculous beings and should proceed with our lives as if we are just that. That is how we proceed here in spirit. We are vibrating at a frequency that allows us to transform quickly, and move through place and time with ease. We are magic and fluid. Even as men and women in physical form we have within us that same being who moves so fluidly so quickly and so wisely through the divine universe.

So, list again the ways in which the world is hard on you and I will list for you the ways in which you make the world hard. It is like a gift that responds to your every whim and fancy. There are men who carry guns and shout out complaints in ways that bring

---

[24] He refers here to *The Secret* by Rhonda Byrne, published in Nov. 2006. Byrne emphasizes the power within each individual to manifest whatever they desire in their lives.

[25] He refers to these words that he wrote in *Walden*: "*The mass of men lead lives of quiet desperation. What is called resignation is confirmed desperation.*"

aggression and force back against them and then they wonder why. In an instant their reality could change. In an instant the intent of the world could change.

"The world is but a canvas to our imaginations." - Henry David Thoreau,
A Week on the Concord and Merrimac Rivers (1849)

EXERCISE OF KNOWLEDGE

What we fail to see in the world today is an exercise of knowledge. It is instead this notion that everyone's truth is valid because it is theirs and belongs to them. Everyone's truth is not valid and true, it is their best guess at times based on faulty material. It is their best guess based on years of wrongheaded thinking. When we can treat a murderer with compassion and as if his crime did not occur, then we have lost our way. We might show compassion for a repentant man, but when we show compassion for a monster and release him back onto the streets to commit his crime again, then we have not acknowledged that for some there is such a distortion from this place of true knowing that they have no morality and will hurt and harm and kill without conscience because they do not understand that there is responsibility and purpose in all that we think, say and do.

It will be a long hard struggle to break away from the wrong thinking that takes from us our ability to discern right and wrong. There is right and wrong, there is right action and action that is wrong and hurtful and comes from a selfish place. That is a fundamental principle that is not being properly acknowledged today and society is suffering as a result.

You must also guard against those who dream so dreamily that they feel that all is well because it is basked in the light of God. All who come into the light of God and do so with open hearts and minds and full intent to connect to truth are joyous and light, but those who are creations of God are not reflections of him when they take part in deeds that are best termed evil. You cannot be forgiven, and you cannot take any action that will be forgiven, if you do not see the wrong.

"Do what you know you ought to do. Why should we ever go abroad, even across the way, to ask a neighbor's advice? There is a nearer neighbor within us incessantly telling us how we should behave. But we wait for the neighbor without to tell us of some false, easier way." - Henry David Thoreau, Letter to H.G.O. Blake, December 19, 1854

THE WORLD TODAY

It is a difficult thing to look upon the world today and see the chaos that continues. In my time we were aware that there were other cultures and countries where reality differed significantly from our own, but we lived with limited news and information in the sense that it was not there at our fingertips throughout the day. Imagine picking up a device pointing it at the box in the corner and a picture displays, and within that picture box are scenes from all over the world - live scenes. We are seeing into a dreamscape of space and time and there are advantages and disadvantages it creates, for none of us is large enough to handle the mass of the world all at once. We can handle merely the small part of the world that we occupy and do what we can from that small space to better ourselves and therefore humanity. That is what I see for I still believe that we are more powerful as individuals than we are as part of the whole.

There is division and disharmony in the world today because we do not yet understand the depth and breadth of who we are inside and seek our identity through exterior roles. We are great because we are members of a race, a tribe, a political party, a church, a company or a team, and we seek to preserve our exterior roles, without ever fully understanding who we are within. Until we recognize the power we have as individuals and the true depth of our souls, we will continue to be nothing but self absorbed hooligans who will do as we please and assert our beliefs and our power over others. We do not have the right to do that in any circumstance.

THOUGHTS

It is easy to allow others to think for you, to dictate your dress, your thoughts, your desires, without ever truly experiencing yourself, because the thoughts and opinions of others are more easily available to you. It is an enormous task to overcome such thinking, for defining oneself as original and unique and working to bring to the whole positive experience and information is to prepare for a wiser cognition and representation of the self.

COMMUNICATION

Man is at his strongest and speaks the clearest when he stands alone and speaks his own thoughts, without care or concern for others thinking. That is rare to find. Most language is cloaked in caution, fear of approval or rejection, fear of wrath or indignation. Few are strong enough to speak their own minds, or experience life through their own sphere of perception. They instead repeat what they learned from a book, a play or a television show. They do not know themselves what they think or feel because they do not ever truly take the time to pause and look within.

It is a more difficult process to convey thought to a man. With man there is an undertow of expectation or judgment and communication is shrouded. We listen, not just to the words of a man but also for his intent, and it is often that intent that we react to and not the words. Do men lie? Men frequently lie, whether aware of their lies or not. This is part of their method of interaction. It is a level of wrong communication, a way to support the process of wrong living, wrong actions and demonstrates a lack of connection to the source.

You can blaspheme yourself and your own life, you can treat others with disrespect, act in violent or obtuse ways, and still in the end the principles remain the same. They are undeniable. They are the same for all. This learned, it would be a different world, for the truth of the light would dissipate the madness.

"Many an object is not seen, though it falls within the range of our visual ray, because it does not come within the range of our intellectual ray, i.e. we are not looking for it. So, in the largest sense, we find only the world we look for." - Henry David Thoreau, Journal, July 2, 1857

"In wildness is the preservation of the world."
- Henry David Thoreau, Walking (1851)

RELIGION

Let me discuss the topic of religion. I was not a Sunday goer, only in the sense that on Sunday I was on the go, usually out of town and away from the churches as swiftly as I could move. The townspeople looked disfavorably upon me for my refusal to become a member of any of the parishes in town, but I knew a greater parish of which I was a member and I saw no resemblance to that within their parish walls.

Waldo, too, who had been raised in a family with a long line of ministers, recognized the ritual and redundancy, the ego inspired truths, the traditions, the losses and lack of resilience that was present in those religions. Let me further explain my distaste of them. Here come our Sunday goers now. Let us step to the side and watch. The women in the best of their few poorly sewn dresses wrapped in shawls and prepared to take seats in their much worn boxes or pews. They are my neighbors, the familiar faces I see each day, grumbling as they go about their daily tasks, the chores, the things they consider difficulties in their lives. They gossip and complain and point and prod, all into each other's business, all into the game of one-upmanship and advancement in material things. I see them clutching their Bibles to them and smiling reserved smiles while hiding their conditions as they listen for hours to the orator who drones on about the God who will save them. That is what I see.

These men and women who degrade and belittle each other throughout the week, collect then on Sunday to be redeemed somehow, as if the words of another man who stands before them could somehow improve the states of their own tired lives.

81

Nothing will improve their lives but a moment of revelation that opens them up to their own true natures and connects them to the divine that is within them. Then and only then is there hope. Without it, there is repetition and displacement and unhappiness in their lives. And they criticize me for my desire to stay clear of them. Why, I wonder, do they not see the beauty that is both around and within them?

THE STARS

As a child I would look up at the stars in wonder and be reminded of the depths within me. We are so vast, even those who think they are only their physical bodies, who think they are that without soul. It does not matter what we come to think of ourselves through the course of our sorry lives, and many of us have sorry lives, difficult lives, lives of abuse and torment and shocking disrespect. Even when living those lives where we are the least that we can be, we are still at core the most that we can be, for we are always and forever spirit.

THE PLACE OF
THE WISE SILENCE

It is in the place of the wise silence that truth is revealed. Meditators sit for hours with closed eyes attempting to reach that place. It is there for all if only they can settle their minds long enough to reach it. It is warm and bright and brilliant, it is all things and all things are it. In that place of the wise silence peace, integrity, and truth exists.

WISDOM

Wisdom is a tricky thing, for it takes you up and out and away from your contemporaries. It gives you a different song to sing and at a tune and decibel that is different than any that has ever been heard before.

"Knowledge does not come to us by details, but in flashes of light from heaven." - Henry David Thoreau, Life Without Principle (1863)

Chapter Nine
Truth and Perception

"...on the spiritual levels all is laid bare."

As consistent as the connection with Thoreau was most of the time, there were occasions when it would drop off completely. I was never sure whether it was a change in me that caused the disruption or if it was simply that he was not available. Who knows what demands are made on us in the afterlife or what other obligations he might have that took him away? My tendency during those episodes was to blame myself for being unfocused or not concentrating hard enough. In fact, when the connection was there and active it took very little effort on my part to connect, and when it wasn't there then there was absolutely nothing that I could do to bring it about. The vast difference in energy that I could sense during those off times was another of the factors that convinced me that what I was experiencing was real because when Thoreau returned it was like a light coming on in a dark room and soon all systems would be go again.

LOSING CONTACT

You leave little time for us today, but I welcome you back, or graciously say thank you for welcoming me. Do not distress over the lack of communication at times or criticize yourself when the communication grows dim. It is not always you but simply a matter of the ebb and flow of the universal energy. The contact will not be lost. We are here in this for the duration. What we will write here will be a treasure for many, a gem to hold in their hands and relate to some element of truth that will flow from it in this world that is otherwise adrift on the falsehoods and fallacies of so many.

THE GAME

Truth has no weight or value to it anymore. The game instead is what can we get away with. If a man can "get away with it" in this day and time, he most likely will. That is a sad commentary on the nature of man and on the lack of connection to soul. As you know, and as we have spoken of before, there is little that we "get away with" on the spiritual levels because on the spiritual levels all is laid bare. That is a true statement. Your friend who wants to write the book about dancing naked is on to something with that title. We are all dancing naked here in spirit, as what we are and what we think and what we intend is there laid bare for all to see. There is no dispute over what is right or wrong or over which man's intentions are best or for the highest good, it is clear. No one can succeed in illicit behind the scenes ways here, there are no behind the scenes. Now this is not to say that there is not privacy. It can be attained, but no one can stand behind the mask they wear. There are no more pretty faces to mask an ugly truth, no more perfect cars any more perfect than the neighbor's, or better homes to prove their worth above others. Here, the true worth of the individual is there for all to see. We are judged here most accurately for who we are. How we feel and think, how we wish to be, and how we wish others to be is seen for what it is. You may have lower thoughts here, but then you resonate downward to lower vibrations and alas lower company. That is the fact of the universe. All that you do comes here with you when you pass, and it is yours to work through, and ultimately we keep the best and discard the worst.

It is not, as you say, all love or any one emotion in particular. That is true. You are wise to recognize that. It shows a realistic approach to what lies beyond, rather than an idealized one. That is true wisdom, not an illusion cast to influence others in a certain way.

Those in darkness will not easily give up the dark. Be prepared to fight a true fight and stand tall. I see now that you are able to do that, once you have stepped beyond your own demons. I congratulate you for the effort you put forth to get past such things. It is not an easy task to overcome yourself. Think not of the past any longer. "Thought police"[26] yourself away from the darkness as much as possible and keep the faith for your work will be known.

At that point I felt a sudden and profound shift in energy. There was another spirit coming forward who wanted to communicate with me, one that required a much deeper level of connection than was usually needed in my communications with Thoreau. She identified herself as a guide of mine who was stepping in to address some of the fears I had in this process.

I had no direct experience with my guides up until that time in my life. I believed they were there and I had a habit of calling out to them now and then - mostly to complain about what a poor job I felt they were doing for me. I had even been so bold on a few occasions as to declare them fired and ask for new guides and now and then they would come through during some of the readings I'd had but usually only briefly to pass on their admonition that I should have more respect for them. This time it was different. This guide identified herself by name and demonstrated her power in the way she stepped in and seemingly effortlessly took over the connection I had with Thoreau. It was an incredible episode, in the midst of what was already an extraordinary experience I was having, and it was the first of what were to be several appearances, or I suspect Thoreau considered them interruptions, by her during the transmissions. She always manifested with a loving energy towards me and in this first

---

[26] During one of my readings with Rev. Barbara in Salem, MA around this time she used the words "thought police". Here, Thoreau is borrowing that phrase from her and I felt as if it was delivered with a wink.

appearance she brought a cautionary message to me about the protection I might need as I continued on this path.

The telephone rang during that first connection with her and I answered it groggily - something I rarely experienced when breaking a connection to Thoreau. But connecting with this guide required a deeper level of energy and concentration from me and it was like being awakened out of a deep level of sleep when that telephone rang. After the call I went back to my desk and tried to connect to her again but she was gone. I then asked, "Henry, Are you there?" and soon after I received this brief and amusing reply from him:

Let me brush off the dirt from my pants that accumulated when I was tossed to my knees in the wake of that hurricane of higher energy. I can do nothing but step aside in the face of that. We will continue later then.

And with that we were done for the day. It was late in the afternoon by then and I had to stop to get myself ready and head on into work, but the following morning, our communication resumed and there was more time to discuss what had happened and for him to express his own feelings about the higher realms and those who reside in them.

I am here, yes, as always, waiting for another chance to resume our dialog. Yesterday was a miraculous day in its way for you, to have someone come in from the higher levels, to remind you of your connection there. The higher levels do exist and as you may gather now, I do not spend a good deal of my time in them.

I am a humble man for the most part, seeking my own truth and my own path in my own time. I do not wish to ascend to the highest heights for I will lose touch then with humanity. That is how I see it. The wisdom of the higher levels is often lost on the ordinary man.

88

Let us continue and we will see how far we get before we are again interrupted, or perhaps we will be left at peace today to do our work in the time we have.

ALTERED STATES

I drifted in and out of full awareness at times, as you yourself do. That was true of me throughout my life. Do not underestimate the impact that nature had on me in a larger spiritual way. My experience with nature was transformative. The awakening of my consciousness culminated in that moment on the mountain that they call my contact.[27] It was a moment that took some time to evolve to. I was not always cognizant of the altered states as you may assume that I was. I was drawn to the natural settings, but not truly shifted or altered by them until that moment on Katahdin. There for the first time I truly understood the altered states that we could go to, if so inspired or driven to do so. It was there when I allowed myself to float in a sense out from my body, to see the distinction between the two, the physical me and the spiritual, infinite me. This dimensional form of existence is very much the true nature of things. There is a dimensional aspect to our emotional structures as well. There is an ebb and flow that may be seen in many forms, how love turns to hate, hate to love, want to need, need to satisfaction. We can move and change our emotions at will. It is a matter of focus and intent but all emotions are waves of one true emotion and that true emotion is an entity in itself.

THE ETERNITY IN THE MESSAGE

There are more things in heaven than our minds at last allow. For the vastness is more than can be described or known and the concerns of any one individual are all at once as vast as that universe and as small and petty and minor as they can be.

---

[27] Here he references a passage from his book, *The Maine Woods* that is commonly known as "the contact passage." See Chapter 28 for a more elaborate discussion of the contact passage.

89

I have invested an eternity in this message. There is an essential truth that lies in my work that must be known, so count these times as blessings then that you in your life have come to a place where you may now receive this message and help to bring it forth to new eyes and new minds and souls.

* * *

FAMILY

Chapter Ten
Biking

"Instead of Walking, I might have written Biking!"

After a year in Bedford where from my favorite spot on the sofa I could easily see the bike path that ran behind the back yard of the townhouse where I lived, I decided it was time for me to buy a bicycle. I had not ridden one in over 15 years at that point, and even then only briefly when I bought one while living in Cambridge and then returned it when I discovered that biking the tight and traffic filled streets of Cambridge was too dangerous for me. I thought then - while in my mid 30s - I might never own a bicycle again, but after a year of watching bikers of all ages and capacities passing by outside I decided to try once more, and it was one of the best decisions I have ever made. Soon I was up each morning, donning a helmet and taking off on my bicycle for what I experienced as sheer joy.

There was a break in the guardrail along the street where I lived that provided access to what is known as the Reformatory Branch Trail - the unpaved path through the woods that runs behind homes in the neighborhood where I lived. In one direction it leads over to Bedford Center where it is easy to connect to the paved and significantly more popular Minuteman Trail and in the other direction it leads into Concord. That was the way I most often chose to go, navigating the sandy trails along the way as I passed beside the Great Meadows conservation area and skirted along the back side of Sleepy Hollow Cemetery. After navigating through some rough and frequently muddy patches, I would arrive at Monument Street near the Old Manse and the North Bridge feeling victorious. Some days I would venture off the path and wind my way around the roads in Sleepy Hollow instead - both the older part where the graves of Thoreau and his family and friends are up on Author's Ridge and the newer section with the wide circular drive. From there I would cross Bedford Street and head into Saint Benedict's Cemetery where the roadway in the newer section at the back provided a large track-like area where I could bike many laps, adding mileage and exertion to my ride.

I thoroughly enjoyed my biking excursions. Meandering around on the outskirts of Concord village, largely unseen or little noticed, while connecting to the gentle energy of the area, filled me with a sense of freedom and joy. It was a wonderful time for me and I would return from my biking excursions exhilarated and anxious to continue my conversation with my friend, Henry. One day I received this acknowledgement that they were in fact watching what it was I was doing.

> We watch as you glide through on your bicycle, this new you who you yourself do not recognize. This is a joyful time for you and we admire that, and encourage it. It is your way of experiencing what I myself experienced in my walking of Concord. I walked everywhere. Every inch of land bore my own footprint, and every sound that could be heard there I listened to with my own ears. Listen as you travel to the sounds around you, not the nagging irritation of modern day convenience, but the sounds of the birds and the other animals who occupy those woods that you pass through. Listen to the creatures of nature and there you will find true heart and soul and remembrance.

At another time I received this:

> In the society in which you now live there is this emphasis on physical fitness. Everywhere you go you see the fitness clubs, and everywhere on the roads of Concord are these fantastic bicycles. I am with you, my dear, what a joyful wonderful event to ride such a contraption. I wish I had owned such a bicycle in my time. Think of

the distance I could have traveled on it! Instead of *Walking*, I might have written *Biking*! It is the truest and most complete sense of outside and adventure and speed and youth. Yes, I see well what you mean by it.

Chapter Eleven
An Ancestral Connection

"I am your cousin, too."

During the same years that I was engaged in this channeling with Thoreau I became interested in ancestry research. I joined the genealogical research site, ancestry.com, and began to create my family tree. With a mother born in England and a father who was the son of recent Scottish immigrants, I didn't expect to find any member of my family living in America prior to the 20th century. Boy was I wrong about that! I soon discovered a fascinating and fruitful line that led me back through nearly 400 years of the history of my family in America beginning with the arrival of the Mayflower in 1621. I was so excited to find that I had ancestral ties to the Mayflower and heavily New England roots that I was soon spending more time investigating my ancestry than I was spending connecting to Thoreau. That didn't mean that he and Brad weren't still hanging around though, or that they weren't also interested in the research I was so caught up in. One day, after an invigorating morning bike ride, I sat down at my computer intent upon spending an hour or so on ancestry research but instead I found myself quickly connecting to Thoreau and I was surprised when the first words I received from him were: *I am your cousin, too.*

I immediately balked at that statement. I thought there was no way that could be true. I must be making it up, and allowing for that thought, I began to doubt all over again in the very process I had proved true to myself so many times. The only resolution for this latest conflict in belief was to search for information that would validate his claim so that is what I did. I began by looking at Thoreau family trees created by other ancestry.com members and eventually I created my own Thoreau tree, hoping that somewhere in the maze of early New England families that I had found myself tied to I would find my ancestral link to Thoreau. It took several days of searching but eventually I did. It was through a set of shared grandparents who were born in Norfolk, England and lived in Plymouth County, Massachusetts in the early 17th century. They were 4x great-grandparents of Thoreau's and 10x great-grandparents of mine, thus making us 5th cousins, 6 times removed.

I was thrilled at having found what appeared to be a verifiable link to Thoreau, but ancestry research is not as easy as it might appear to the uninitiated. Claims made on sites like ancestry.com are not always verifiable in actual records because hundreds of years ago they were not quite as diligent about keeping vital records as they are today, not in the U.S. anyway. That was the problem I ran into with the ancestral line that had led me to Thoreau. According to H.W. Brainard, a well-known and respected genealogist of the early 20th century, the link was there but I could not find any actual records that would back up his claim. I spent several hours one morning searching through records at an old town hall in a small town in Connecticut, hoping to find a record that would confirm my tie to the great-grandparents I believed I shared with Thoreau. Many of their descendents were buried on a hillside nearby, including their great-granddaughter; the woman who I needed to prove was my 7x great-grandmother. I found no records that morning that supported that claim, and later that same day the clerk at the much larger town hall in Willimantic, Connecticut invited me into the back room to look at the original handwritten entries in a large and quite old record book in order to prove to me that my 6x great-grandmother was not in fact named in the list of children of the woman who was buried on the hillside a few miles away. I left feeling disappointed and defeated.

About a year later I returned to that same small town in Connecticut, along with a distant cousin from Michigan who I had met through ancestry.com. He was one of the many cousins I had communicated with online who were for their own reasons trying to prove this same grand-parental link that I was. We found a few items of interest that day but none provided the verification we needed. Still Thoreau insisted he was my cousin, not just in the problematic link in New England but also back in Scotland where we shared other ancestral ties. I have yet to investigate whatever records may exist there.

For those who wonder, yes, I have in fact connected psychically with some of the ancestors who have come up in my ancestry research, and some, with the assistance of other psychics, have been quite helpful. In the case of this particular missing link, confirmation was received through spirit that in fact the connection is there, but it seems, at least as of this time, that there simply are no records that exist to prove it.

* * *

Chapter Twelve
Family

"I lived in a world full of love."

After our ancestral ties were revealed, the transmissions from Thoreau turned to his own family and the relationships he had with them. In many of the transmissions he seemed determined to correct some of the misunderstandings about his family members, his mother in particular, who is often written about unfavorably by Thoreau scholars as being overbearing and gossipy. Thoreau seems to have had a different experience of her. He also addresses some of the ongoing criticisms of him having to do with his choice to remain living in his family home.

A   WORLD   FULL   OF   LOVE

I lived in a world full of love. That is what you must tell them. I lived in a space so sacred and real to me, for even in my darkest days and even in the times when I would wish to have freedom from them, I knew them to be the truest friends and the truest loves to me for they were my family. I lived in that time and that mind set always.

It was in childhood that I found the truest peace I think I ever felt. It was in the joy of playing – bounding across the fields of Concord - living to see and explore all aspects of nature. There was no greater joy in life for me.

FAMILY

It is true that I was a man who never left his family home. I was tied so tightly to my family and their needs that I never imagined a life for myself without them. Perhaps it was because their home was in fact a boarding house that it remained my home after the age when I might normally have moved out. Had I found housing at an adult age, I might well have moved into a boarding house in town. As my family home was that, I simply stayed put. That is one way to view my inability to swim upstream and spawn, so to speak. Instead I resided there with them and witnessed the slow devolution of the family I so loved. We were a hardy and happy group of people.

My mother, who is known for her overbearing and loud personality, was at heart a kind woman who rarely scolded, but more offered loving reassurance and compassion. I did admire her as the strong woman she was, but also was aware in part of the impact that strength had had on me. My father had learned to be a silent passenger on our family ship with my mother at the helm, and I suppose that worked well for each of them, as it allowed her a forum to express herself and allowed him the peace and solitude he needed. It is not so unusual for couples to compliment and accommodate each other in that way.

There was a level of love and trust within my family that was unsurpassed I thought in many others. We were a kind lot who treated each other with respect and support, always. It was our great and good fortune to have such a mother as ours who looked after us so diligently. It made up in some regards for a father who was somewhat less attentive. It was not that father did not love us. I think instead he felt encumbered somehow by the presence of feminine in the home. He spent a good deal of his time away and preferred the conversations he had with those he met on the streets of Concord than he often did within his own home.

Our family unit was a strong one, and when the first death came, that of John, it was a devastating blow to all. I believe that father felt the blow the hardest, perhaps next to me, as he saw in John a man he could truly admire, one who would have, had he lived, married and had children and carried on the name of Thoreau. That was what a man would do and that is what father expected would come through John. When John passed, so quickly and so painfully, it was devastating for all of us. I don't think father could believe that that son had gone, and he was left then with the women, and with me. He always saw in me that I did not fit as other men do, and he never fully came to terms with that. He was not an intellectual man. He was more of a simple man with simple attitudes toward life. My books that later were regarded so highly were never of great interest to father. I do not think he ever understood me. That is not so unusual for a father and son, but still he was a kind man and I do not demean him in any way.

My sister, Helen was the other star of our household - this bright, passionate woman, who taught school and who fought hard for abolition. Had she lived there would be more written about her, the fight she waged to free the slaves, and the struggle she would have fought in support of woman's suffrage. That would have been her destiny, but again we lost her to that plague of our age, the tuberculosis. I know now of course that she was witness to all the events that came after, but we would have benefited from her continued presence there in our family and in our lives.

PASSING INTO SPIRIT

With Helen's loss, the family was dealt a severe blow because we were now a gathering of four and not six and later we would become a gathering of three, with father's passing, and later of two with my own passing into spirit. I do regret the sorrow that rang throughout the house on the day I passed. Mother and Sophia were there next to my body weeping for their dear Henry. Little did they know that I stood there beside them, reveling at my new juxtaposition and at the immense vibratory sense of the energy that surrounds. I took a last and final sweep through the town of Concord and then lifted up and away into this place where I now reside, into this magical spiritual realm.

Do not ever consider that I stayed in any kind of ghostly form, for I did not. I was happy to be free of that retched body upon my passing and as I have already described, I rejoiced at the sights that were waiting for me, as young Wallie stood so ready to greet me, and soon, too, my brother, John came round, and then father standing like a bold brave force against the backdrop of eternity. Those were the images that greeted me upon passing, and Helen later found her way to me. What a loving warm light she is as she resides here still, contemplative and sorrowful in a way, but still learning, always learning, even as she rests.

C O N C O R D

Arising to the smell of bread baking was not unusual as it was a daily habit in our home to make bread. We had not just the family, but our boarders to feed, so it was a busy kitchen that mother and my sisters held there. Drinking tea with a slice of hot bread from the oven, and later, with an apple in hand, walking out onto the streets of Concord. That is how I remember it, walking down Main Street toward the center of town, amid the dust created by the horses and buggies going by. It was a dustier life then that is for sure because we did not have this thing called pavement that covers and destroys the earth. I prefer a little dust to that concrete monstrosity.

The welcome I get in town is rather a curious one. Some who say hello and smile quickly avert their eyes so as not to confirm my existence, but make haste to fulfill their own obligation of courtesy to another. There are those, however, who show little courtesy to me, and I let them pass, not so concerned with their lack of reply to my greeting or the greeting they expect from me that never comes. Their opinion of me little matters for I am considered an outcast by so many. *"Where are you working today?"* would not be an unusual question asked of me. *"Work?"* I reply, *"Work is for the unwise and unoccupied."* They think what I do is for the shiftless and unmotivated.

MUNDANE LIFE

I did not find enjoyable any aspect of mundane life. I never did. I mean it was a comfort at times to sit at home and allow my family to cater to me and that was a pleasant experience, but beyond that, to the effort that often went into preparing and maintaining a home were to me utter boredom and something I wished and often did my best to avoid.

There was the pencil business that I worked at with my father. It is known that I was able to perfect a type of lead and I found it fascinating in my efforts to find the right composition that would produce such a product. There was an element of creativity involved in that endeavor that I found appealing and enjoyed but once I had done it I had no desire to do it again because my desire was always first and foremost to add to my base of knowledge and once I had achieved the perfect pencil, then I did not need to pursue that skill any longer.

It is as I expect I would have felt, and others may find themselves feeling, when they take on something like marriage or fatherhood and establish for themselves their own family. For after a time they might wonder what they will do next, now that they have done that, but then they realize that the endeavor they have engaged in is for life, and so there they sit.

You must forgive my limited views on such matters, but I speak in truth about the position I took then. I was no more fit for the pursuit of marriage and family than I was for any other aspect of domestic life. I simply did not have it in me, and so it was not meant to be.

I chose then to find my own way in the world, without venturing too far. I kept to the narrow streets and paths of the town I was born in and soon my life began to expand before me. Soon I understood what it was I was there to do.

* * *

POLITICS AND
PURPOSE

Chapter Thirteen
The Politics of Thoreau

No,... I will not write another essay!

In the fall of 2007, an announcement appeared in the Thoreau Society Bulletin about the theme for the following summer's annual gathering. The theme was first listed as *The Politics of Thoreau,* but later it became *"The Individual and the State: The Politics of Thoreau in Our Time."* My first reaction when I read the announcement was to ask out loud, *"What politics of Thoreau?"* and then I began spouting my objections, knowing that Henry and Brad were sure to hear me as they were always lurking about in those days. I went on about how Thoreau didn't have any political beliefs and about how his views continue to be misunderstood, even, I dared to assert, by the society that was founded to honor him over 50 years before.

I was quite animated and impassioned, but let me put this in context. We were about a year into the transmissions at that point, and yes, I had learned a lot along the way, but nothing I had learned so far could account for the insights I had into Thoreau and his work that I was brimming over with in that moment. I was talking about *Walden* and about the essays he had written. In particular, I was talking about *Civil Disobedience*, something that I had never read before, at least not with clarity of any kind, and yet I suddenly knew it inside and out. I was going on about Thoreau's true intent being spiritual, not political, and about how he was asking for a better government, a government with a conscience not no government at all. I went on about this for several minutes and then, just as quickly as I had started, I stopped. I sat down on the sofa, picked up the remote for the television and began searching for a good movie to watch. All I wanted to do was to relax for the evening, but Henry and Brad weren't going to let me off that easily. I could sense that they were there with me, waiting patiently, while I slowly figured out what it was that they wanted me to do.

"No," I told them in no uncertain terms, "I will not write another essay!" and I meant it. I hated writing them. The one I had written to honor Brad that was published in the Summer 2006 issue of the Thoreau Society Bulletin, an issue that was dedicated in memoriam to him, was the first essay I had written since college days and I had never been any good at them. I was surprised when long-time Thoreauvian, Robert N. Hudspeth, who had taken over as editor of the Bulletin upon Brad's passing, had been willing to publish it. That had gotten me excited about writing more of them but all of the others I sent to Dr. Hudspeth in the months that followed were rejected as too speculative for the Bulletin. This had left me frustrated over the amount of time and energy I had put into them and I could see no value in writing another essay that would not be published, but Henry and Brad assured me that this time it would be different. This time my essay would be published and in it we would take on this notion that there ever was such a thing as "The politics of Thoreau".

With that I gave in. I mean what else was I going to do? I picked up a pad of paper and a pen, and while still comfortably situated on the sofa (my small protest as I was unwilling to go to the computer to connect in the usual way) I asked them, "*What do you want me to say?*" and then I made a list of each subject and sentence that came into my mind. This was a much more casual and relaxed style of communication than it was when I was at my computer and it was the first of what would be several occasions when we communicated in this way. It was also around this time when I began to connect to them while in my car and I bought a handheld tape recorder so I could record the words I received from them as I drove. It was 2007, not everyone had a cell phone that recorded back then.

Those moments when I was fully relaxed, eyes open and just talking to Henry and Brad in the most casual way were the ones that I most enjoyed. I could ask a question and the answer would just come to me and the more animated and lively I was during those conversations the more fun it was for me. I relate to those in spirit just as I do anyone else because we share one common denominator - we are all spirits - whether or not we are occupying a physical form. And, to be clear, I am not saying that I heard them in any kind of traditional auditory way, either in this casual style or when I was at the computer. In my experience with talking to spirits the communication takes place telepathically. I listen with my mind and soon their words and ideas are there, but when I speak to them I do it most often in the traditional verbal way. I believe it is the intent behind the words that is heard and understood by them rather than the actual words I am speaking, but I am not 100% certain of that.

In any case, for a week or so they conveyed the basic themes and a fair amount of the text to me and for the next two weeks I wove it all together to create the essay that was entitled, *The Politics of Thoreau: A Spiritual Intent.* Dr. Hudspeth responded almost immediately upon receiving my submission, and, just as Henry and Brad had told me he would, he accepted it for inclusion in the Spring 2008 issue of the Bulletin, which came out just before the gathering that summer. I had few comments from other Thoreau Society members about the essay but those I did receive were all complimentary, and the gathering went on as planned with several lectures focusing on Thoreau's political views. They even had a keynote speaker that year who addressed the crowd about anarchy - painting Thoreau in the same role he is often and so wrongly placed in, as anarchist. How this opinion was ever derived from his essay, *Civil Disobedience*, is beyond me. In *Civil Disobedience*, Thoreau clearly states, *"But, to speak practically and as a citizen, unlike those who call themselves no-government men, I ask for, not at once no government, but at once a better government."*

In that single sentence Thoreau identifies himself as a citizen of the United States. Would an anarchist identify himself as the citizen of any state? And he makes it clear that he is unlike those who call themselves no-government men. In other words, and in his own words, he is telling us he is a government man and thus, he is not an anarchist.

Thoreau addresses the issue of anarchy in the following transmission:

MY CRY FOR DEFIANCE

There are those who believe that my greatest gift to this world was my cry for anarchy. Decry the government, all governments, and instead follow who, me or yourself? No. I do not, nor did I ever, make a plea for anarchy. How could I make such a plea? Why would I? I was a fond supporter of the United States of America whose very existence had first taken rise in my town. I respected the founders and the principles they relied on as they formed the constitution. They believed in a divine creator and in a government that represents and serves the needs of the individual, not a government that acts for and represents its own needs.

What I wanted was a government with a conscience, one that has its own direct connection to the divine, and conducts itself accordingly. I wanted the same thing in man, and believed that when a man found that the actions of the government were not aligned with what he knew to be true based on his own connection to the higher laws, then he should have the right to disobey.

I spoke of peaceful disobedience and believed the individual had a right to express his opposition if done in peaceful ways. It is not the right of the individual to come in full force with guns blazing against the government, to act in effect in the same coarse and crude manner that the government itself would act in order to enforce its own unjust laws. By acting in that way the individual has stooped to the government's poor level. The rights of the individual are supreme when the individual is acting from a place of divine right. When aligned with the divine, he will chose then a course of peaceful resistance, peaceful disobedience, and fight with the greatest strength of any man and that is with full faith in himself and what he knows to be right. That is not the same as an individual who acts out of ignorance or misinformation and chooses to fight the government shot for shot. That would not be right action, and would only bring more ignorance to the scene or subject.

9 1 1

There are those who will reject this notion of the individual acting out of the faith he has in what is right and wrong but when I speak of Right Action I am speaking of an individual who acts from a true connection to the divine. A true connection to the divine does not result in the kinds of violent acts that are perpetrated upon others in this world in the name of God. It is clear to all who look upon such acts that they are wrong action. No action that stems from a true connection to the divine would result in the devastation and destruction that came from what is considered the 911 conflagration. Those men, although determined and confident in their own beliefs, were not acting from a true connection to the divine. They were acting based on the precepts outlined for them in their religion.

POLITICAL PARTIES

I have not the need to define myself as a member of a political party and do not understand why others would do this. To give allegiance to one party over another, one group of thieves versus another, is enslavement of a certain kind that does not allow for my own freedom and self determination and so it is worthless.

GOVERNMENT

We are not in debt to our governments; we do not need to breathe our every breath for their cause. What cause would a government have that would be my cause? A government is a body of individuals nothing more, but that body government and the majority that elected it are as easily at fault as any government could ever be. Without a conscience, without its own connection to the higher laws, then there is no government whose laws I will respect more than the divine laws that I myself have the power to perceive.

PRESIDENTIAL ELECTION - NOVEMBER 4, 2008

It is a grand and great moment for all of us who are here now who were there then in those times when men like him, who were good of heart and God's creatures, gentle, kind beings, were held in shackles and forced to do manual labor for no wages, beaten and abused and sold as property to the highest bidder. That is what we saw then, what I saw with my own eyes, and now this. My emotions rise in surprise and joy that a black man could be voted into the presidency, but in reality what do we have? We still have just a man.

In this time of great change in this country there is the need for a deeper view of all things, and a serious view, for there is in this time of media a desire to build one up to heights not before seen and to admire him and reflect upon him all of our hopes and dreams and to do so with blind vigor.

There is great hope with this man, but if his message is simply "through me" then the message is wrong. It is through you, and you alone, each individual, that you will find truth, it is not through any government, or any President who represents that government.

ECONOMIC CRISIS - 2007/2008

We watch as the economic structure of this country begins to crack, all at the fault of those who were so materialistic in their endeavors, so unwilling to think of anyone but themselves, and who risked all for their glorious income based philosophy. They value their property, more than they value their own souls and they thrive on taking more and more when they should be having less and less. They drive the best cars and think they are better; they live in the finest homes and think they are better. They do not recognize the weight that their possessions place on them. I found myself burdened if a simple sea shell should come to occupy its space with me. It was me and the body that contained me that I most cared about.

In my assessment of the world at this time I see few who have anything of real value. Many still think possession is king but perhaps that is the lesson of the times, as through their financial losses they are now forced to rethink their own value and to look more closely at their empty, shallow lives. Many of those individuals when they cross will not expect to see grandness so many will not. They will shiver in fright until someone they know ushers them forward, and then they will soon begin to see just how small they were in life and just how much bigger they are destined to be.

* * *

Chapter Fourteen
Putting Pen to Paper

"There were changes within me, and changes within the system."

"Seeds, there are seeds enough which need only be stirred in with the soil where they lie, by an inspired voice or pen, to bear fruit of a divine flavor." -- Thoreau, A Week on the Concord and Merrimack Rivers (1849)

In addition to his book, *Walden,* Thoreau is best known for his essay, *Civil Disobedience,* but there were many other essays written and lectures delivered during his lifetime. The best known and most relevant to the following transmissions are: *Civil Disobedience* (a/k/a *Resistance to Civil Government*) (1849); *Life Without Principle* (1863); *Slavery in Massachusetts* (1854); *A Plea for Captain John Brown* (1860); *The Last Days of John Brown* (1860); and *After the Death of John Brown* (1860).

S L A V E R Y

When a man puts pen to paper in response to any injustice he takes on a great responsibility. His thoughts will be measured against the injustice and whether he is perceived as wise or faulty, in his own or others judgment, he is allowing the world to see his descent. That in itself makes it a difficult and courageous act. It is easier to stay at home silent and not speak out against injustice, because if the majority of men support the injustice, whatever it may be, then that majority may turn against anyone who dares to speak out against it. That is the point at which those of us who fought against slavery found ourselves. The majority of men and the federal government supported this institution called slavery, and although the abomination of the institution was clear to any who could see, there were few dissenting voices at first, few who dared to speak out and say that it was wrong. Of those few who did they were criticized for their sympathy with men who were savages. That was how this race of men was viewed. They were savage men because they did not speak our language, and because they lived in conditions in their native lands deemed uncivilized before being transported here against their wills, treated like animals and used for hard labor.

This great abomination was allowed to go on in this country unchallenged for some time before the first of the voices came out against it. There was too much at stake for many to defy their own government, too much at risk for them to dare to defect. That is the power that the government has over its citizens. As long as the citizens will not risk the peace and comfort that they cherish, then the government can act without cause in any direction it chooses.

When I put my pen to paper and began to speak out against the injustice of slavery I found myself with greater self esteem than I ever had before. Until then I was merely a teacher. That was in itself a good occupation, but not one that so overly fulfilled me. I felt more fulfilled when I began to write my truest thoughts onto paper and deliver those thoughts to an audience who might never have heard such opposition before. I built a reputation for myself in the small communities where I spoke. My reputation was as an eccentric man with views outside the norm, whose anger over a particular topic at times distressed my audiences, but I believe I sparked something within some of them, certainly on the issue of slavery. There were times, however, when not all of my words were understood by my audience and I walked away wondering why I bothered to speak at all as many had lost my meaning as soon as my words were uttered.

I did better with the words that I put on paper. I expressed my views and I encouraged others to do the same. That is what I most pride myself for - that I encouraged constructive action in opposition to injustice, not hostility and revolt for the sake of hostility and revolt. In putting pen to paper I took responsibility for my own opinions and put them forth confidently as my own and from that intent to influence the masses against the injustice eventually change occurred. There were changes within me, and changes within the system.

Putting pen to paper is an act of pure fate in some regards, but a powerful one. There is no doubt that with words we can influence and change the world, and that is what we seek to do again here.

HEROIC PEOPLE

Those I knew who put pen to paper in my time were great, heroic people, who were viewing life outside the traditional mold. They were not the people who were lining up for church on Sunday mornings; they were people who had the courage to look with clarity at their own truth and who dared to speak out against injustice and to help to bring about change. It was a grand journey, as it remains today, for those who chose to undertake it.

Those of us who followed the transcendental ideas were trailblazing in the midst of advances in science and scientific perspectives. Science would eventually become the dominant view in this country and relegate the area of belief strictly to that practiced in the church, while dismissing those as frauds and charlatans who dared to speak of spirit outside the confines of religion.

UNDERGROUND RAILROAD

There is much asked about my participation in the Underground Railroad. Of course I acted in whatever ways I could to protect those individuals who sought freedom in the north and in Canada. I did and would of course do whatever I could to help. This was not something I felt I could not do. It was something I felt was mandatory to do. Did it matter to me that I was breaking the law? Of course not, for unjust laws made by an unjust government are not laws that I, as an individual who is in touch with my own highest guidance, would ever follow. I did not obey the unjust laws of an unjust government. I chose instead to act in ways that were consistent with what I knew to be true.

* * *

Chapter Fifteen
The Mission and the Misfits

"There is a larger purpose to our lives that we do not always see."

I often use the word "misfit" to describe myself and others who live their lives outside the norm. It is one of the things that most appealed to me about Thoreau when I was first reading about him decades ago. He was always the rebel, always, as he described in *Walden*, *"walking to the beat of a different drummer"*. This is a characteristic that Thoreau and I share and I believe it was a characteristic of mine that he had to grapple with throughout this process. I was always determined to do things my way, in spite of what he or Brad might have in mind, and it didn't always work well for the overall goal of our shared mission. In the following transmissions Thoreau talks about his mission and about us misfits

THE MISSION

I do not wish to be known as a man who did not fulfill his mission in life, and I believe that sometimes I am seen as that. I died young, that is true, but I had walked many miles, studied many aspects of the physical world and when I expired I had a greater understanding of life than when I began.

I wish I could have stayed longer, but the rewards of my passage were equally as wonderful, because of the depth of knowledge that exists here within the spiritual realm for those of us who desire to discover and learn. We are occupied each day in our excursions on this side and continue to learn and grow in every way, so there was no loss in my dying then, and no tragedy because it was a mission complete.

There is a larger purpose to our lives that we do not always see. Whether it takes a man 85 years to complete his mission or 45 or 25 is not relevant in the larger scheme. When the job is done, then we are ready to ascend to this spiritual place, and that is what we do. This does not make it any easier for those who remain behind, but just as we have shared our love and support with them while there we do continue to share our love and support with them from our place in spirit, whether known or unknown by them, and the sense of loss, however painfully endured by those who remain behind, is quickly dissipated upon their reunion with their loved one in spirit.

The fact that Thoreau was talking about issues of aging and length of life in that transmission was no surprise to me. I had recently been spending too much time dwelling on my own age. I was 48 dreading 50, which seemed like a big deal to me at the time, but my focus on the mundane while in the midst of an experience that was as remarkable and magical as this one seemed to disappoint Thoreau. He did not understand the dichotomy in my thinking, and would frequently point it out to me.

TURNING BACK

There is no turning back, no getting younger again in that body. That body will age, but you as a soul are steady and permanent and powerful and wise. I would wish to see your recognition of that fact more rather than your focus on the physical form. You exhibit the gifts of awareness and yet conduct yourself at times as one unaware. We mystify about that. It is as if you are wearing unmatched socks. We like to tease. That is the case, however, when one side does one thing and one side does the other. There needs to be more synchronous action between what you know

122

and what you do and there needs to be consistency in your thought and practice and in the words that flow from you.

And, as if the "unmatched sox" comment wasn't teasing enough, there was also the playful puppy remark that came during a reading with Rev. Barbara in Salem around this time. Their concern centered around the habit I had of running ahead of the throw, so to speak, like a playful puppy who was eagerly anticipating the ball. I was well aware of my tendency to run with an idea once planted, rather than wait for the words that would follow, but they were always quick to stop me when I did, so I am not sure why I needed the reminder. Maybe they just liked the image of the puppy and were having a good laugh at my expense? Later, I was told:

Do not judge too harshly anyone and do not judge so harshly yourself. Think instead of a grander ideal and go with that, for that is how the grand state of being will be allowed to be experienced there. You must act it to feel it, or at least try. You attempt instead at times to hide it and that is not the way to help yourself or anyone else understand. This is your reality. It is one in which you were destined to live and you must obey the flow of the wave that takes you to it and returns you from it. Alas, these are recommendations and observations, not commands from on high. I do not consider myself on high, I do not make commands. I believe in full responsibility and self determination.

With that remark both Thoreau and I could sense a change in the energy again, a deepening that allowed for my higher guide to once again speak through. It was not lost on me that she chose that moment as her message to me was both of protection and encouragement as I was continuing to let go of some of my more negative patterns. When she departed, Thoreau returned with the following remark.

This higher spirit is always something that leaves me in awe as she floats so freely in and around us. I find that I experience utter bliss when I allow myself to ascend to her realm and experience her reality. She seems today to find bliss at the level where we connect.

You should remember, however, that when it comes to our observations of the world, from this position we don't always have a full view of things, and there are many mysteries about life that elude us here.

THE MISFITS

It is one thing to say that I was a misfit and did not long for society, but as you know there are layers to any reality and the reality of solitude is the constant longing for companionship, but fit companionship is not easy to find. Not willing to suffer fools is a characteristic we share. We do not have time to waste in endeavors for the sake of companionship, so we choose instead our solitude or the company of things or places or nature to enchant us.

To spend your days in company with someone who does not stimulate your mind or awaken a revelation within you is wasted time indeed. You will find I expressed this widely. I learned more in simple solitude and reflection and while in connection to the grander universe than I did in hours spent with anyone who was unaware or unknowing. In your novel you describe so beautifully what it is like conversing with those unaware.[28] You cannot be heard by those who do not have ears and you will not be heard by them. You will however be heard by many who will understand and who will resonate to your message and if you can hold on to the satisfaction that may come from that, then you will do well.

Ultimately, it is how your work will withstand the decades after you pass that will be the true test. Who better than me to address

---

[28] Here he is referencing a line in a novel I have written but not yet published. Evidently he had some means of access to it or simply read the thought as it occurred in my mind.

that reality? I had so little success, and a good deal of criticism in my time. The criticism came from all directions. You think you suffer inside as one who walks down the street, not quite fitting, feeling always a sore thumb in the company of others, I felt the same sense of revolt in combination with hurt that you do. We are misfit, unfit for a place in society, so we are left outside of it looking in and wondering at its value, wondering why we are not a team to it, and yet it is us who are the lucky ones. We are forced then to see the grander picture and we find in that the greatest comfort there is.

"The question is not what you look at, but what you see"
- Henry David Thoreau, May 6, 1854.

"We must look for a long time before we can see."
- Henry David Thoreau, Journal, August 5, 1851

Chapter Sixteen
Criticism

"...there is never any glory in putting down or tearing down another,
there is only difficulty in it."

"As they say in geology, time never fails, there is always enough of it, so I
may say, criticism never fails." Thoreau, Letter to Ralph Waldo
Emerson, February 20, 1843

In August 2007, I read an essay about Thoreau that was written by biographer, Joseph Leon Edel (1907-1997) that was published in his American Authors 90 Pamphlet Series (1970). In that essay, Edel takes a very negative view of Thoreau, his life and his beliefs. I knew little about Edel at the time. His name was only familiar to me because of the book he had written entitled, *Bloomsbury: A Den of Lions* (1979) that had sat on my bookshelf unread by me for many years. It was one of dozens of books I had collected when my literary interests were primarily in the writers of 1920s London and Paris and not yet the transcendentalists. When I learned that Edel had written an essay on Thoreau, I knew I had to read that essay and I was about three-quarters of the way through it, eagerly consuming every page while voicing my objections to Edel's remarkably negative take on Thoreau into my seemingly empty living room, when I felt a familiar pull that led me back to the computer where I once again tuned in and received this transmission from Thoreau:

You have been reading the words of a man named Edel. I have since met this man as he passed into this world of spirit and we had a laugh or two about our subjective opinions of each other. What a dark and crude sort of man I thought, to take after me with such hostility, to feel he must prove the worthlessness of my cause and position, the falsity of it, or what he presumed was so false, and to speak this venom so articulately as to impress so many and destroy so much. Well, that was my experience of him. Still he points out much truth in demystifying the myth of me and my own mystification as I created a book about my journey. This is not unsaid before in this book, still again I will say there is a mystification and glorification in some cases as an artist works. Are the paintings of the impressionists less valuable because they capture the feeling and sense of the scene rather than the precise detail? I suspect not. There are many who take wealth from those impressions. The books I wrote are my own impressions.

Professor (how I hate to use that word) Edel is but another in a long line of hyper-critical academics who never quite get to the truth of the matter and poke and prod at those of us who somehow do, as if pointing out the flaws in our characters or our work will somehow reinforce their own vague belief that the truth cannot be found, is left for a time in the afterlife, or does not exist at all.

That is my experience then of Edel and so we are equally opposed to one another, and equally accepting that we had borne those conditions, and entered those minds. It is experience, interaction and interplay; it is life as we lived it, and as we continue to live. He is off somewhere. We still do not readily relate, but there are many who do.

Who, but you and a few others recognize the name Edel? But who does not recognize the name Thoreau? That I am proud of, and why shouldn't I be? I fulfilled a mission to leave the world with a message and I am pleased to see that the message endures and the name endures and that men like Edel by comparison retire relatively unnoticed and unadmired. It is difficult to admire someone who takes for himself the position of scourge against another. This is a difficult position to take. I occasionally took it myself, but there is never any glory in putting down or tearing down another, there is only difficulty in it.

The following transmission was directed to me as Thoreau addressed the criticism I might be facing with the publication of this book. It was just one of many times that he spoke to me directly about that kind of thing. He seemed to be genuinely concerned about my well-being throughout this process and aware of the challenges that might come as a result of my publishing such a book as this. What follows may be the most important bit of advice I, or anyone who dares to present themselves and their work to the public, will ever receive.

PUBLIC CONCERN

There is an element of privacy that is lost with each part of yourself that you publish. That is fact. Each part of yourself that is put out for public consumption takes away a bit of you. You must know then that you are not your work, and you are not this public image of you. If we were that, if I were that, then I would have long ago been consumed and destroyed.

I have not yet decided which it is that causes me the most concern, the ridicule that I endured during my life and that I to some degree continue to receive today, or if the public adoration that continues is more harmful.

I am aware, fully aware of the adoration that comes up around me, particularly in the academic circles in which I myself would not count myself a member in my lifetime. I do not wish to be admired in the way that I am by many, because many of those who admire me do so with false ideas in mind. I have to remember then that my life was cast out before me and I followed the path, did the work and then I left it all there for others to take from, and they made it and me into what we are now. It is separate and apart from the real me, the true me, and that is what I fight and what you must fight to preserve.

You do not have to grant anyone permission to know you or to see you in any certain light. What you must do is paint for them a picture of yourself that they can then invest their interests in and protect for yourself the part of you that is most sacred and humble. Let them cast their spells around the image and not around the true you.

***

Chapter Seventeen
Idolatry

"I am not God, I am man."

The Thoreauvian community is split into two camps, the enthusiasts, who I count myself a member of, and the academics, who, in my opinion, most often are the least creative and the least interesting of us and yet they dominate most of the annual gatherings and many of the local events, as in fact they did on October 14, 2007, in a presentation at the Concord Free Public Library.

Many of the usual local Thoreauvians were there that night, including Ed Schofield, who, the following summer, would give me a delightful tour of Thoreau's Worcester on what was one of the hottest days that year.[29] I was seated next to Ed throughout the lecture as I listened to the academics proclaim their latest victories in their ongoing research on Thoreau, a man that they mutually worshipped.

I am not entirely immune myself to the hyper-idolization that so many there seemed to be experiencing toward Thoreau that night, but as the speaker began to discuss her analysis of Thoreau's original journals and gave a slide presentation illuminating in detail the precise location in the journals where Thoreau had written certain words, even reporting on tiny marks he had made with the slip of his pen, I looked around the room at everyone there who seemed to be

---

[29] See Chapter 23 "Touring Thoreau's Worcester".

so completely engrossed and wondered if we hadn't all lost our minds.

I'd had a similar reaction to one of the first Thoreau Society annual gathering lectures I had ever attended. The presenters had gone on at length about the need to investigate and accurately footnote all references in Thoreau's work that were not readily understood by most readers. They were determined that not one simple syllable of Thoreau's words would be left without clarity. I found the prospect of that kind of research to be tedious and boring to say the least and when I told that to Brad at our first meeting at Lesley University in 2003 he had laughed out loud at what I am sure he recognized as a thought that was had by many but was rarely expressed. Then he joked about his own lack of life due to his devotion to Thoreau, but of all of the Thoreauvians, I believe Brad was the one who was most adept at bridging the two sides of the Thoreauvian community. He was an enthusiast bar none but he had also accomplished much that pleased the academics, and he had done this without ever truly becoming one of them. He was greatly missed by them though, and each time his name came up during the lecture that night, and it came up several times, I wanted to reassure them that Brad was neither dead nor gone, and that it was very likely that he was still assisting them with their work whenever he could, if only they would open themselves up enough they might be able to see that.

At the memorial service held for Brad during the annual gathering the year before, Brad's closest friends, who I was surprised to find were not at all Thoreauvian, had talked about moments when he had been so taken by the insights he would have into Thoreau that he would have to drop whatever it was they were doing so he could record his thoughts. His wife had also spoken about a time she remembered how happy Brad had been when he rushed into their home one day excited to tell her about what he believed to be Thoreau's fingerprint he had discovered in a book Thoreau had once checked out of the library at Harvard.

I have to admit, finding something like that fingerprint might have made me ecstatic, too, and in truth, defining and identifying misunderstood references in Thoreau's work might have some value, but I saw no value in examining the tiny marks Thoreau had made with his pen in the journal, or why he had written that word in that place or chose to use it in that way. All of that was the kind of thing that academics loved to spend time on, and it all seemed absurd to me. I sat down at my computer when I got home that night and soon I received the following:

ONLY GOLDEN

There is so much focus on the minute and the silly. I am but a man with a pen in my hand, that is all. Not every mark that comes from that pen is brilliance. To idolize me is a mistake. I was a man, that is all, and a famous one now and the message that is the most important is somehow lost behind my name. "*I read Thoreau*" is a grand pronouncement for many, but the true accomplishment should be, I understand his message, I incorporate it into my own life and now it is mine. The message is not me. I myself am not the message.

It is simply absurd to cling to my every utterance as if it were gold. I am only golden on Tuesday and Thursday. Laughing. I am only golden after Sunday morning tea. The rest of the time, I am working things out. Now this study of how I worked things out, this will feed the frenzied and famished academics for all time to come, and let them have it. Let them gnaw away at the bark of the tree while you are getting about the business of sawing the wood and making a fire that the whole world will see.

Their microcosm of microcosms will impress few and enlighten no one. I myself could not tolerate such delinquency, in the form of mastery. I do not refer to the reading of my manuscripts and perfecting them for publication as Brad has done. I refer to the over analysis of the scribbles that are meaningless. Why must they know or care how I constructed the entries in my journal? What is the meaning of the words I said? That would seem the most important point.

It is wrong to think that I walked with a halo or that light spread out from my limbs as I passed through town. Quite the contrary I am sure. That may have been Waldo's mode in town, but it was not mine. I was dismissed as inappropriate for my age, immature, irresponsible and illogical for my lack of choice to conform, but I demonstrated that for some there can be another path, for we are not all born to conform.

It is true that I wrote those words about hearing a different drummer.[30] We must be allowed that. The individual is his own best master and must be the one who ultimately decides his own fate. It is wrong to impose our own views on another in any form, and, if I stood out as a model for anything, that is what I best modeled. It is the most important idea of my own.

If a man lives to carry the message of spirit to the mass of men who are so in need of it and so lacking of it and a light comes on inside of them when they hear it and they are reunited in effect with their own connection to source, then let them honor the spirit within them and not cast praise and lavish adoration upon the man who delivered the message. The greatness and grandness is with spirit, not with me.

I am not God, I am man. I am the conveyer of the message, I am not the message. So, there again is the first and most important message I share. It is not the messenger who is the great one, it is the message itself that is great and you, and all of you know this.

Thoreau may not like the idolatry that is directed towards him, but he did have his own heroes. Abolitionist, John Brown, was one of them. In his essay, *A Plea for Captain John Brown*, first delivered as a lecture in Concord on October 30, 1859, soon after Brown's arrest, and just over a month before Brown would be hanged for the violent tactics he used during the battle he waged

---

[30] "If a man does not keep pace with his companions, perhaps it is because he hears a different drummer. Let him step to the music which he hears, however measured or far away." Henry David Thoreau, Walden

against slavery as an institution and those who held slaves, Thoreau made these statements about Brown:

"I rejoice that I live in this age, that I am his contemporary."

"This man was an exception, for he did not set up even a political graven image between him and his God."

*"He shows himself superior to nature.
He has a spark of divinity in him."*

Thoreau, A Plea for Captain John Brown (1859)

In a transmission received a few days after the initial discussion on idolatry Thoreau responded to the questions that I had about his defense of such a violent man as Captain John Brown:

DEVOTION

I believe John Brown was a true and devoted man, acting out of his own deep connection to the divine. I believed it then, and I believe it today. Is there anyone who questions whether his goal to free the enslaved oppressed people was a noble one? Are there any who believe that he was wrong in his desire for that? I do not think there are many, if perhaps one or two odd and off souls. It was clear to any who had heart that this act of enslavement of any individual was wrong. I chose to speak out in support of Brown and did so with no regrets. I believed in his cause so fully and whole heartedly, but my support of him has cast doubt upon my commitment to my own beliefs. For my act to support this man who was in fact so brutal in his attempt to rid the country of this scourge of slavery, has cast a shadow of a sort over my own reputation that remains today. Let me attempt to clarify my position.

IDEALIST

I was an idealist in many ways. I could see with such clarity the true principles I believed in and I felt compelled to live by those principles as best I could. I could easily be swept up in the excitement and vigor of another's determination toward a goal I could relate to, and I could relate so strongly to the goal of abolition.

I supported in full measure Brown's desire to abolish slavery in this the American land. I was not aware of the extent of the barbarous methods he would chose to achieve his goal. However, in principle, I did agree that in some cases the loss of innocent life might be needed to save a greater number of lives. I believed that in principle. I did not advocate for it, and I did not and would never chose it if given another option.

It was a matter of weighing one evil against another and proceeding accordingly. So I did not fault my friend, Brown, and I continue to feel that his slaughter at the hands of the slaveholding government was an abomination and a merciless death for a man who fought so gallantly for such a worthwhile cause.

I have not seen him here since I passed. I do not know where he is or might be. I do not wish to imply a hellish region here. There is none here that would match the evil place depicted in the Bible, yet there are those dark and strange and horrible places that anyone can create for themselves, if desired. If you expect to find hell here or there, you may well find it. I do not know what my friend Brown found when he passed. I do not know where he is and have not the knowledge to convey. I suspect he may have returned to life again, to live as a free black man. I would hope that he might but I do not know that as fact.

* * *

Chapter Eighteen
On the Subject of War

"In some ways it is as if such wars were needed."

"War educates the senses, calls into action the will, perfects the physical constitution, brings men into such swift and close collision in critical moments that man measures man."
- Ralph Waldo Emerson, Journal, 1828

One day in September 2007, the tone of the transmissions changed. I knew it was no longer Thoreau who I was connecting with but I did not dare to believe at first just who it turned out to be. The revelation of who it was sent me into whole new levels of doubt and disbelief as I found myself asking why Ralph Waldo Emerson would be talking to me. He began with this:

E M E R S O N

What is war? What is this thing that causes so much pain and suffering? It does that, does it not? And yet from this side, the pain and the suffering from the physical side quickly dissipates and though we do not discount the seriousness of the pain felt, it is transitory in nature as are all things and we arrive again at start, at the core of who we are, at this greatest level of being and from here, such matters become less severe. That is, they are merely experienced on a broader canvas and we are able to see a

*longer and much truer path. But what is the value of war?
What is this thing we do?*

*No, this is not Henry. You are quick to assess and recognize
that. Today you are speaking to me. I am not the old man I
was at death. I am a live and lively spirit. I have lived many
lives, not just the one of Emerson, and I am alive still and
witnessing and observing contemporary times.*

*I am smiling at your reaction to me. Why be it this way
when we are so close in thought? When you address me
with such reverence each time that you speak of me and
hold me in high regard? There is nothing in your manner or
your intent toward me that I would have need to address,
but instead I thank you for the long standing respect that
you offer me. I am, as you say, considered similarly by
others as well. They hold me in high regard because I
always held them in high regard myself. Those who came to
me for counsel, who sought my wise admission into their
lives, I treated with respect and understanding and I believe
that is why I was regarded well. I also lived in step as much
as I could within the society of the town that I loved.*

*Your friend, my Henry, he was not that way, and as he has
already confessed to you, was a man quite distinctly
different than the others. He would have been always cast
aside from society at whatever time or age he would live
because it was his nature to hold himself apart, to see
himself apart, and that is in fact how you, too, view yourself,
but not for the same reasons, perhaps. But Henry is the one
who deliberately sought not to conform and who spoke out
against such conformity and looked down his nose at those
of us who did conform. It was a reaction, a retaliation of
sorts, if you will allow for such words. He was our radical.
Step away from the beaten path, and find one of your own
then Henry, but never show your weaknesses, never allow
the weakness that you possess as a man to show, give it*

another name and allow it to be known and recorded as another more noble reason for the path you chose. Never admit that you were simply unfit for the roles that others of us played. That is how I saw and continue to see it, and as you have already heard from him, he sees it to be that way as well.

I do not mean to degrade or humiliate the man who was such a dear friend. My children continue to love him and loved him all their lives for the bright light he brought to them, the wisdom and kindness, this talented, extraordinary man that he was. Now you see that I also recognize the brightness in him. There was sheer joy within his heart when interacting with the children. That was something he attempted to retain all his life and it was only in the last few years when the illness became too much of a burden that he lost any of his natural playfulness. But Henry was and remains a joyful and determined soul, simply miscast for society's ways and that I am sure was no mistake. The impact he has made on the world is great, greater than mine I will concede in many ways, because he appeals more to the common man, while still conveying this all powerful message that we are one, that we are all born of the same one, and we cannot change that fact, however isolated we attempt to become, however rare we are to society.

Henry approaches now to continue this dialogue. I do want to affirm that you have a worthwhile subject in our friend, Henry. I thank the Gods for allowing me to live in such a place and at such a time as he and the others and as you yourself live, now and then. Blessings to you and stay with this project, polish it and perfect it and make it worthy of the consideration of the masses that will be caused to change their own attitudes as a result of your work. Listen to the call within your own heart to assimilate more to those around you, to the place where you live, and to all aspects of life there on earth. I step back then and allow our Henry to continue. We will speak again later.

THOREAU

I will not waste time taking offense to Waldo's remarks about me. I am laughing. He is still such a proper man, and I am still just me, just Henry. He is right to say that in my interactions with people I was less than cordial, less than proper, less than accepting of who they were, because it was all I could do to be me. That may surprise some, but I was always there having to deal with Henry, as we each have to contend with ourselves, and as one who stood out so from the crowd, I was there with my pride facing the arrows shot out toward me. I was never a welcomed presence in Concord, not in the way Waldo owned the town. He was the hierarchy in town and I a son of one of the less mannered families. That was somewhat true in our status. I am laughing again as here we are not so status conscious.

Waldo wants to speak on the subject of war and he wants me to address it as well. We do not necessarily see eye to eye, but I will talk briefly about the subject of war. Waldo is taking a larger view and seeing it as a function, a way to work through our differences. The natural expression of man is violence then? I would like to say and behold to all that the true nature of man is love, and when at the core that is what one truly feels. Again, let me address the question that is asked about those men on the planes on 911. According to what I have written, they should be in the right because they were acting in accordance their own deep devotion to God, but the men who drove those planes and thought themselves devotional were far off the mark of true enlightenment. True enlightenment never includes the killing of others in the name of God. True enlightenment comes when we connect with the divine source of all and feel the purity and power of the love that exists there. I believe that is the true nature of the universe, compassion and love, but there, in the physical, there are

140

only glimpses of divine love, and the love we share between us is a poor comparison.

The physical world is a place for souls to work through their negativity and in some cases, their positivity. We are all "at work" there. That is hugely ironic for me to admit and it brings an enormous laugh from Waldo. Me and my talk of devoting as little time as possible to work, now that is ironic for it seems I find that life by its nature is work, and is meant to be so. The physical realm is not a playground, it is a workground. It is a place to experience all that one can in the physical in order to learn and to grow and so it is by its very nature, work. Even in our most pleasurable moments we are learning or teaching and growing on the soul level.

So as we discuss the topic of war, and reflect back over the centuries of war on this planet, and the wars that take place elsewhere in the universe, we can see that war has its function or else we would not have it. It is part of this workground, part of what we experience here to learn and grow. I do not advocate war, but if challenged, if threatened, if forced to fight back, then I do, then yes, if fighting for the proper cause, then I do. But how do you identify the proper cause? Isn't our enemy's cause the proper cause, too? All of this is so complex, and yet so simple. It is the experience of an actor in a play. I am playing my part, my enemy is playing his and we battle it out to the end, and in the end we reassess and we see what we have learned from the battle and then we go on. None of us is trapped by any of the roles we play and all of us are immensely larger than any single expression. We are forever. The word forever comes up loudly here. We exist forever.

EMERSON

I would like to speak about war, but I do not wish to linger over what is a heavy subject and I do have my own reputation to consider. I am laughing, but it is true in some

141

regard. In this time that you live should a sentence appear that reads that Emerson comes back from the grave and says something in support of war, now then I would have a predicament. They would take away all support they once had for me. Now let me clarify my position. In an ideal world, when true wisdom comes to each individual then we no longer war. That is plain and simple. In that ideal world there is no need for it. But there is not at this time an ideal world. I will report from this level that there is not an ideal afterworld either. There are those levels in spirit where the wars of earth are continued, soul against soul, fighting out the same differences in politics and beliefs that they fought on earth. In some ways it is as if such wars were needed.

I do not see any resolution of war or ridding of the planet of it until all men have reached a level of peace within themselves and know and recognize each other as sharing the same inner core. For now, and until then, we have opposing forces, and like the hot and cold forces come together in the sky to produce thunder and lightning, the opposite forces of belief and philosophy will come together on the earth plain and the result will be war. There is unfortunately a need for this hashing out. There is a need for such battles to be fought as we work our way to a greater understanding. We do not simply stand up one day as children and walk across the floor. We take many a tumble before we have achieved our ability to walk. We are learning. The physical plain is a place of learning. We must understand then that those who are there are there to learn, and some of the lessons are large and involve many.

Blood was shed in this country in my time when we fought hard against a great evil. So many hundreds of thousands of young men died in that war, and in a brutal bloody way. Houses are built now for the wealthy and their well fed children on the land where men in my time fought and died. They fought hard and they bled hard and eventually justice won out, for the brutality of slavery was then abolished from this land. It is hard to look back on that war and not say that it was worth the battle. Would it have been better had it not had to be fought, had all men seen that slavery was wrong and agreed to free those men and women who were being held captive? That would have been the preference, but in this world, then and now, things are not that simple.

There is a need in many for a broader understanding. Those who live without knowledge of the spiritual will act out of emptiness and their lives will be empty in same. They will act upon poor influences, and "react" instead of "right act" and war will often be the result. There is a greatness that we are all a part of and those who are lost in the present are unaware of this greatness. They must find their way back to it and they will not find their way through the media that is so laden with lies or through their technologies that serve only to distract them. I do not know how a society still stands that is so laden with putrid device, profanity, and pornography. I am driven to shouting at this disgrace. How do you treat yourselves with such disrespect? How do you allow such degradation of your souls to exist? How do you live and look at yourself in the mirror and mistake the reflection for the real you and try to conform that reflection to ten million other reflections that are neither them nor you? Why do you continue to offend your souls with these misguided notions? These are the truest signs of a degraded society when value is placed on the reflected image and never on the soul. This must change. You must remember your worth. You must look within to find your truest selves and act based on the wisdom you find there. That is when you will experience wholeness in your life and wholeness in the world and not the fragmentation, disgrace and self-loathing that permeates the world today. The wealth is in the one and in the whole. Whatever we do for ourselves, we do for all.

"When will the world learn that a million men are of
no importance compared with one man?"
- Henry David Thoreau, Letter to Ralph Waldo Emerson, June 8, 1843

THOREAU

As long as it is the will of a government to create war and the will of men to fight it then there will be war. Yet, I stand with those who fight against it and ask for sanity in the face of insanity and think that perhaps if we chose another path, then another path would be revealed to us. But, what can a man do if he is warred against? I say to that, we must fight back. Complex issues like this do not always have remedy on the earth plane.

"I do not wish to kill nor to be killed, but I can foresee circumstances in
which both these things would be by me unavoidable."
- Henry David Thoreau, Plea for Captain John Brown (1859)

* * *

Chapter Nineteen
Education

"...he must do it on his own, with his own mind, which is his own device."

In the fall of 2007 an email was sent to Thoreau Society members announcing a call for papers for the upcoming American Literature Association (ALA)'s annual conference in San Francisco, California in May 2008. The topic for discussion was to be "Teaching Thoreau in the Twenty-First Century" and as I had already received so many transmissions about education and teaching I was sure I could put together something that would appeal to the ALA. Writing all those essays the previous year may have made me over-confident because I had never written any kind of academic proposal before, I lacked the academic credentials (i.e. M.A. or Ph.D.) that most members of the ALA had earned and I knew I was going into territory that I had never been comfortable in, yet I went ahead with it because I had one major thing going for me, I had Thoreau around to help me to write it.

At the time, I thought that writing the proposal I called "Teaching Thoreau to the IPod Generation" and submitting it to the ALA was an opportunity for me to begin to share some of the information I had received in the transmissions but I sensed very little enthusiasm from either Thoreau or Brad on this effort. I was surprised by this because from the time of that first reading I had with Rev. Barbara at Angelica of the Angels in Salem, I understood that education and teaching were to be an important theme and purpose of the "excursion of books" that she told me they, Henry and

Brad, wanted me to write. Rev. Barbara's use of the word "excursion" in that first reading was one of the things that convinced me that she was indeed talking to Thoreau and to Brad. It is a very Thoreauvian word and one they must have known I would recognize, but I found it as daunting a prospect then as I do now to write a series of books about the writers of Concord in any traditional academic way. I am not now nor was I ever a traditional scholar of Thoreau, and yet writing the proposal for the ALA seemed to me like something that I could do. Still, Henry and Brad offered me no encouragement. I thought maybe that was because writing the proposal took so much of the time I had so little of, but I realized later it was because they knew that whatever I wrote was not going to appeal to that academic crowd. Thoreau had this to say about the ALA.

> You elect to write this paper for the ALA, such an organization I would have ridiculed in my day. Their bale of attempts to understand me contains nothing but dry straw and worthless properties. You cannot gain nourishment from them.

I was intent though on drafting a proposal and determined and confident that what I wrote would make an impression on the ALA members in spite of Thoreau's low opinion of them. As I did, more transmissions from Thoreau on the topic of education came through that I incorporated into my paper. I present some of those transmissions here, along with quotes taken from Thoreau's published works that I found years after the transmissions on education were received and that confirmed and validated the ideas contained in the words I had received from him. This had occurred in other areas of the transmissions as well and I included those quotes sporadically throughout the manuscript, but nowhere was it more evident than in the passages I received on the topic of education.

WHAT IS EDUCATION?

> What is education? The attendance for certain hours within a classroom where we learn to dot the I's and cross the T's and reproduce for our teachers the answers to the questions they

present to us. So limiting an experience that is, and so limiting that type of education. No, for me education is a broader experience one that comes through life of course, but also through books that appeal to our curious minds, intrigue us, and draw us in. I prefer the harder choices when it comes to reading. This seems a lesson worth considering in this modern time, when it is so easy and effortless to find things to occupy us. The most frivolous and ineffectual information is consumed while the more powerful and notable works get little consideration, because they are more difficult to receive. You must choose what is best to broaden the mind, not to deaden it. Seek knowledge, not entertainment. Choose those things that are worth your time, and that value and respect you and your life.

"We are all schoolmasters, and our schoolhouse is the universe."
- Henry David Thoreau, Journal, October 15, 1859

READING

We were better readers in my time, more thoughtful, more desirous of what lay before us in our hands. We treasured every word of the books we owned and were apt to sit for hours with them. They were the only means we had then, short of our own imaginations, to be taken away and shown other places, other people and other cultures. We were limited and yet, the hours I spent reading enriched my life for the rest of my life. They were not a simple hour or two spent in front of television before bed, they were hours spent taking in information that helped to shape and form me. They built my character, rather than detracting from it.

The act of reading has become a chore now and other methods for taking in information like the television, the radio, and the internet have become more important because they are the fastest way to get information, and yet they lack the richness of the experience we had with our books. You cannot consume only the light, easy and unchallenging and expect it to feed your mind. It will not and soon your mind will atrophy and your powers to think will be lessened and gone. Ask more of yourself and more you will have.

"Certainly, we do not need to be soothed and entertained always like children. He who resorts to the easy novel, because he is languid, does no better than if he took a nap." - Henry David Thoreau, A Week On The Concord and Merrimack Rivers (1849)

A BOY WITH A WATCH

I see a young child coming out into the sun from his home where his mother and his sister occupy their time in household chores. I see him walking with a book bag in hand to the nearby school where he must learn his education. There is little in the way of gadgetry in this school and many of the fundamentals we teach when it comes to science are basic compared to what is known and taught of science today, but this boy, a boy in my own class there at the Concord school stays in my mind for his brightness and the energy that was all about him. He has his paper, his pencils, and a watch so he can see the time, and to use for amusement across his desk. He does not have something called an I-Pod to distract him or even a calculator to figure his math for him, he must do it on his own, with his own mind, which is his own device.

My message for the students today is that they must stop and realize that within them are the tools for the finest in mathematical and scientific computations. There are also the tools for communications on all levels, as you yourself have proven through your ability to connect to me in this way. Except for the device that you use to record these thoughts, our communications are generic and mind-to-mind or best said spirit-to-spirit and there is no need of technology for that. So, for the boys and the girls today, the young people, I would say there is a lack of awareness of this principle that within them is the power to do all of these things. In fact, the objects they hold in their hands, the calculators, the cell phones, the I-pods all of it was first only an idea in an otherwise unfettered mind, and that idea-ologist of that device was using only his own mind to come up with the ideas to grow such a treasure.

I say treasure because I admit that even I as a youngster would have been fascinated and would have enjoyed the play that comes with such devices, at least initially, but as with anything that is manmade and that is repetitive it seems to me I would have grown bored with it.   There is nothing too captivating for me in mechanical repetition. I am a purist in that sense and prefer pure communication. It is better to watch live music let's say, than to experience it thru a device with a thin wire and ear piece that is plunged into your head.

E - M A I L

I do not object to the opportunity for composition that exists in an email exchange. In our time much of our communication was done in short missives, but ours were on paper. Scratch a note down for Mr. E because I knew my aunt was to pay a visit and I was not heading that way that day. So, my aunt would be my transporter and Mr. E would receive my message and later upon her return I would often receive his reply. It was our email exchange, and was our way of confirming engagements or conveying new knowledge, often through written letters and notes because we did not have this electrified device on our desks or on our laps that we could input our words into and press a button to send. How miraculous it is that such devices exist today. I rejoice that they do, truly I do! I find it fascinating that man can have such tools for expediting expression, but then I realize as I look at all such devices that I was in fact correct when I saw that the more comforts and convenience we were supplied, the less of our true selves would be known.

What I favor is true experience, reflection and revelation and not manufactured, reproduced and artificially prepared experience. The difference between seeing a beautiful tree or mountain scenery as it is displayed on a television screen or computer monitor is a long shot from the true experience that one would have with such phenomena if within the scope of its energy.

There within you is the heart and the soul of all things, and you can achieve greatness through your own silent and momentous endeavors, without any device to transport you. Within you is the true treasure and the key.

TEACHING

PREPARING THE STUDENT

We can only teach as much as the student is ready to receive, so you must always prepare a student before introducing him to the words of any man who lived so far outside of his own place and time. This has always been so. We could not engage our students in Concord to embrace the ideas of anyone from the distant past without first informing them in some manner as to who these men were and why they did have relevance.

The preparation in any good classroom must also include the setting. Are all seated in comfortable manners, can all hear and see? Has there been an exchange between teacher and student that puts all at ease? That too is important for preparing students to learn. You cannot take command of a class as a commander at battle ordering students to form straight lines. This is not a good manner in any institution and certainly not in a school where students must be relaxed in order to learn. The more comfortable the student is with his teacher, the more that student will learn from that teacher. That is evident in all cases.

"I would make education a pleasant thing both to the teacher and the scholar. This discipline, which we allow to be the end of life, should not be one thing in the schoolroom, and another in the street. We should seek to be fellow students with the pupil, and should learn of, as well as with him, if we would be most helpful to him." Henry David Thoreau, Letter to Orestes Brownson, December 30, 1837

TO THE STUDENT

If you are to understand my message then you must not expect you can hear it if the television is playing in front of you, or if you have a radio or computer commanding your attention all day. You must set those things aside, at least for a time, so you can make contact instead with the wisdom that is there within the quiet of your own mind. The sky is the limit to how great you can be, and to the revelations that can come to you. For you are free in that state to see and to know all that there is to know.

Have I your attention then? Have you tuned off the radio? Are you thinking not of your girlfriend or boyfriend or your mother or father or the disagreement you had with your brother or best friend? Are you thinking not about the car you want to buy or the new music CD or about the other aspects of the world that are there to distract you? Are you listening closely then? For if you are, and if you listen that closely and wait and pause and let yourself drift, you will find there within you the place of the wise silence, and you can linger there for as long as you will allow yourself to, and you will learn from that silence that there is more, much, much more to me and to you.

All of the key points that had come from Thoreau were included in the paper I submitted to the ALA in January 2008, but within two weeks time I had my rejection. Neither Thoreau nor Brad seemed surprised by it but I was disappointed and all my feelings of insecurity and incompetence, when it came to my ever becoming a part of the academic world, returned to me. Whatever it is that I sense within myself about that world must have come from a prior life, for there is a part of me that longs for it and greatly misses it. I have even flashed back at times to a life I spent living within the comfort of university walls, but Thoreau, who attended Harvard University in Cambridge, MA 1834-1837, had no respect for institutional education either then or now. Shortly after the rejection I received the following transmissions:

UNIVERSITIES

I laugh a bit at the word scholarly, as if something that is "scholarly" or "academic" raises its value over something that speaks the truth. I will opt for the truth every time, well written, but truth. Just because a man stands before you with a degree and speaks on a topic that he claims mastery of does not mean that he is in fact master of that subject. There are institutions in place and there are those who know how to move within the structures and confines of those institutions and gain positions of prominence while having little if anything to truly teach. That was always my disgust with the university system and it remains true today. I believe a man learns more through his own self-education, through perusal of books he seeks out on his own, then when he is prisoner in a classroom for a certain few hours a day and must reiterate and regurgitate the words that are conveyed to him, so that he might please that professor and receive a high grade. This is what it is like to educate within the system. I did not support it then and do not support it now.

THE ACADEMICS

There has been and will always be the need for some to take a simple concept and make it unsimple, to make such complexity as to defy simple logic and by doing so create a matrix for others to follow and while they follow feel themselves superior somehow that they might be capable of following this matrix designed for them by this, some may say, mastermind. I laugh at all of it, of course, as you do, too, because we see that this trip that the one takes the other on is so strange and unnecessary, for the answers are usually simple and there before us, but instead they seek a more mysterious route to them. What could be more mysterious than the ultimate result of our journey, when we truly find that which is within us? That is when the mystery begins, but this manner of getting to it, this desire to build immense structures, or create wildly complex religions with traditions and rituals and rules by which we must live in order to be considered as divine and worthwhile.... I laugh at these, because of course we are all already divine and worthwhile, as by our very natures we are thus.

Simplify, simplify![31]   I meant this in our material needs, our own appetites and consumptions, and in our use of our time. I also meant it in our need for explanation. There is that saying *the meek will inherit the earth*. I would like to say, the simple will find the truth, for it is not hidden and it is not kept under lock that requires only a certain key to open. It is there within all of us, if we only pause long enough to look and to see.

So let the academics weave their vast roadmaps to this simple concept, and we will instead speak it again with more simplicity than ever, and perhaps point out the flaws in their own flawed thinking. They take so many switches and turns that soon the simplest of meanings is lost and they have instead puzzles to depuzzle and spend their time on, while we on the other hand, spend our hours happily in the simple truth of knowing. Those who seek to complicate things, seek to derail us from the truth, because they care more about the complexity and showing themselves of superior mind, than they do of any truths.

"What does education do? It makes a straight-cut ditch out of a free, meandering brook." Henry David Thoreau, Journal, (1850)

"Men have a respect for scholarship and learning greatly out of proportion to the use they commonly serve." - Henry David Thoreau, A Week on the Concord and Merrimack Rivers (1849)

REMINDER

You must remind them... They need only themselves and their own eyes and their own minds to read and comprehend my thoughts. If they are true to themselves then they will be true to me. Are my words so hard to understand? I think they are simple.

---

[31] Reference to one of the quotes Thoreau is most famous for from *Walden*.

But alas, there will be few who can follow a more difficult path, so I advise students who stay within the system to retain their powers of discrimination and supplement their professor's instruction with instruction of their own. We must take responsibility. We must learn for ourselves.

"It is only when we forget all our learning that we begin to know."
- Henry David Thoreau, Journal, 4 October 1859

SPEAKING MY OWN TRUTH

Chapter Twenty
A Strange Tightrope

"It is a strange tightrope to walk."

In 2008 there was a change in the frequency of the transmissions from Thoreau. I had decided to self-publish my first book, *Honor in Concord*, and researching my options, finalizing and publishing the manuscript, and then seeking out opportunities to market it, all while continuing to work full-time in Boston, meant I had little time left to sit quietly recording the words that were sent to me. On the occasions when I would connect the transmissions I received related more directly to events that were taking place in my life at that time and many included some astonishing revelations.

The transmissions I received also addressed some of the concerns I had as I went forward in a public way for the first time with my book, *Honor in Concord*, a memoir in which I shared several unusual but true stories, not the least of which was when I wrote about how I had astrally traveled while meditating and found myself in 1842 witnessing Hawthorne coming out the back door of the Old Manse in Concord (and looking up and seeing me there, too).

I have had many experiences in my life that challenge the common understanding of what is real and possible, and one day, after I had published *Honor in Concord*, and was contemplating how I was ever going to gather enough courage to publish this book with its unusual premise and containing so many more unusual but true

157

stories from my own life, I received this bit of advice. I believe it came from Brad not Thoreau.

> There are those who will accept your story as real because they *see* as you do but there are many who do not. They will think you have gone round the bend. I laugh at this, but if you produce a book that contains the wisdom others wish to convey but rarely do then you will have won the prize. It is a strange tightrope to walk, but in the end, what can you do besides speak your own truth? I mean, really, what else can you do?

So, in this section I call Speaking My Own Truth I have chosen to share many more unusual stories from my life that occurred at the time of the channeling or that relate to Thoreau or this experience in some way. I hope that by doing so I will encourage others to talk more openly about the experiences they have had that expanded their views of reality, or, at the very least, that they will feel slightly less loony in this world that still dismisses such experiences as fantasy.

* * *

Chapter Twenty-one
Into The Astral

"...I will open the door and let you see."

"Concord is just as idiotic as ever in relation to the spirits and their knockings. Most people here believe in a spiritual world ... in spirits which the very bullfrogs in our meadows would blackball. Their evil genius is seeing how low it can degrade them. The hooting of owls, the croaking of frogs, is celestial wisdom in comparison."
- Henry David Thoreau, Letter to Sophia Thoreau, July 13, 1852

In that quote taken from a letter he wrote to his sister, Sophia, Thoreau makes it clear that he had little sympathy during his lifetime for individuals like me who had the desire or the ability to communicate with those in spirit, but given the timeframe when this letter was written - four years after the incident in Hydesville, New York that many site as the beginning of spiritualism in America - it is not surprising that he would have been this skeptical. With his reference to "the spirits and their knockings," Thoreau is making what must have been a common reference at that time to the claims of the Fox sisters (Leah, Margaret & Kate), who in 1848 claimed that a spirit that occupied their home in Hydesville was communicating with them by rapping out answers to their questions about the afterlife. The news of this event spread rapidly in the media of the time. The Associated Press, more commonly known today as the AP, had been founded two years earlier in 1846, and once they picked up the story of the Fox sisters it quickly became a national phenomenon. People came from all over to Hydesville, NY to see the home in the hope of witnessing the rappings themselves and having some of their own questions answered. Although the Fox sisters were later discredited, in part by Mary's 1888 confession (later recanted) that it had all been a hoax, she and her sisters are nonetheless credited with initiating, or perhaps just accelerating, a widespread interest in spiritualism in America and in the United Kingdom.

The spiritualism of the 19th century later became what is commonly referred to as the new age movement of the 20th century. I was first introduced to the new age community in the Boston area soon after my arrival here in 1984 when I discovered Unicorn Books, a metaphysical bookstore that at that time was in one of the older homes on Massachusetts Avenue in the center of Lexington, Massachusetts. It was at Unicorn Books in Lexington where I had my first astrological reading with astrologer, Jan Brink, Ph.D., who had also come to Massachusetts from Michigan, and who was in my opinion one of the best astrologers in New England at that time or any. It was her insightful analysis of my own natal chart that first convinced me of the validity and importance of astrology and inspired me to study it myself. Astrology confirmed for me everything I knew to be true about myself but had been taught to deny, including, most importantly, my psychic abilities.

After Unicorn Books moved from Lexington into an old Victorian home in Arlington, MA, it became my spiritual home base. I would go there often for readings; to attend the classes they offered on a range of metaphysical topics; to browse their selection of books, or simply to take in the calming energy, while petting the resident cat that was most often found stretched out near the window. Most of the astrology books I own and treasure were purchased at Unicorn Books. It was a unique and beautiful place and the time I spent there in the 1980s and 1990s was transformative for me. Those were the years when I was slowly but surely awakening to the reality of spirit, to my own psychic abilities and gaining a better understanding of what Thoreau stated in *Walden*, *"The universe is wider than our views of it."*

In September 2007, I received the following transmission from Thoreau about such spiritually inclined bookstores and about spiritual practitioners in general.

SPIRITUAL BOOKSTORES

I wish there had been such places in my time. In my time we had the ladies who practiced the mystical arts, but they were shunned from the village as outcasts and downtrodden, and thought to have somehow reached the darker side. They were much the same as those in your time who have awareness and abilities and who desire to learn and know more. I had the same desire but I practiced under this thing called transcendentalism. It provided a wide cover for those of us who had an interest in those metaphysical practices.

We did not count among us the soothsayers and prophets, the fortune tellers with tarot and other oracles, or the astrologers, although we were fascinated by them. I am sure that we knew that there was much truth to what they were supposing, but we hesitated to join their forces, as we had suffered enough criticism and disbelief cast upon our own odd course. So, we did not welcome them, although I think we considered them distant cousins.

I am afraid I was enough of a scientist then myself to dismiss their actions. I see now that there are valid methods to reach into the spiritual side. Look at what is taking place here. Could this have been possible then as well as now? Of course it could. Those who claimed to have heard from me before may well have heard for I did attempt at times to reach others who might carry a message for me, but none of them carried it quite as well as you are able to with your means of transcribing.

* * *

Those early years in Massachusetts were an important part of my life as I matured and evolved. I learned meditation at Unicorn

Books and developed a semi-regular practice. I found myself naturally adept at what is called lucid dreaming, having the ability to "awaken" within a dream and take control of it, and also at astral travel. For me, astral travel is a type of out-of-body experience that involves a separation of the consciousness from the physical body for the purpose of observing and experiencing what exists beyond what is considered the normal range of perception. I have experienced astral travel primarily as an ability to psychically see into the spiritual realm. I have also had the experience of travelling there.

Determined to stay connected, both to Thoreau and to Brad, and to fulfill my role in the task we were committed to, I became more and more adept at slipping past the confines of this physical world, and moving freely into the realm that they occupied. One day, as I sat at my desk, eyes closed and connecting to Thoreau, as I usually did, I found myself first seeing an image of and then suddenly present at Walden Pond as it was during Thoreau's time. As I experienced this astrally, I continued to transcribe Thoreau's words to me. What follows is that transmission.

MY ASTRAL JOURNEY TO WALDEN

You are going so deep now into this magical world. You are seeing Walden as I knew it - still the bank there, but no boathouse, no cement benches, just the grassy wooded slope down from the dirt tracks that marked our road past the pond. That is what you are able to see. There was a fallen tree there that lay near the pond where the children and others would sit. I remember it that way. I go to it in that way, that is what is so remarkable here. I can go to the pond as it was in my day, see it there and attend to it there, without the mass of people who are there today. I am as appalled as you are by the number of people who clamber there, all anxious to put their bodies into the pond. It is a polluted space now that so many have come. In my day the water was crystal clear and blue. It was alive with the fish and the nature that surrounded it. I would watch the animals when they came down to the water for a drink or in their attempts to find food, and I see that again any time I go to the pond.

You can see my cabin there on the slope in the cove site they named for me. You know the spot well, but see it in my day and you will see something else. There are far fewer trees of that you can be sure, and I could hear the passing wagons on the nearby road, and it was a shorter clearer walk somehow to where I planted my bean field. Do you see the cabin there as it was in my day? It is dirty from the mud splashing up when it rains. I am not the diligent sweeper that I made myself out to be, but it is clean enough for one guest, or perhaps one or two.

I will open the door now and let you see. The arrangement is similar to what the replica contains, but look closer and you will see my things, my shoes, my books, my writing pencils. Do you see the spot there by the stove where I dropped the burning piece of wood? What a shock it would have been to lose my home in that way. Look below now at the containers that store my stock of food. It is rough and rugged space for one such as you to imagine an underground storage for food, underground where the bugs and the rodents can get at it. That is what you think. You would not have felt that way if living in our modern world. My mother's kitchen was cleaner than this, but not so free and readily available.

There is a crack there at the edge of the window. I did that backing up too quickly with my chair. Something I should repair, but never do. The warmth inside is sometimes stifling, that is how warm it becomes, so I open the door and let in some cool air but at night the fire goes down as I sleep so I must sometimes rise early and replace the log, or risk becoming too cold. These are the simple tasks for my life then, and not so much to handle for one. Here at Walden I am free to read and write and rejoice at simple freedoms. It was and will always be a special place for me.

It was Christmas 2007, when I found myself astrally back at Walden again. I was only there briefly just long enough to see and sense the lovely image I was presented with. I remember thinking at the time that it was Thoreau's way of sending me a Christmas card.

CHRISTMAS 2007

Let's follow the path that leads around the pond when the branches of the trees are weighed down with the snow. It is a beautiful site. I love to remember it this way when the snow lands and the air cools and the sounds soften and there is quiet and peace and solitude. It is winter at the pond.

Look up as we come into my cove and you will see my home and the spiral of smoke that rises above it. Beside it a deer stands alone in the new fallen snow - gentle, kind friend. This is my home at the pond. It is the only home that I had to myself in my entire life. There I picked up a pen and wrote and remembered and thought and desired and related to this world that was around me. There I became the man I was destined to be.

* * *

As the transmissions continued, my ability to travel astrally became a key element to maintaining my connection with Thoreau and with Brad. I had discovered that I could astrally travel to where Brad was and that he would be in the places I created for us there. One spot that we returned to frequently was a mountainous setting, a place I called The Summit. It was exceptionally beautiful with glorious mountaintop views in all directions. I believe it is a place that exists, not just in the astral but in the physical world as well, but our visits there were in the astral. It was a fascinating process, not unlike a lucid dream, but to me it was more luminous and real. Here Thoreau remarks about those astral travels that were frequent at that time.

There are those who can orchestrate their lives in this way - draw a picture on a canvas and watch it come to life. It is so much that way in this spiritual world, so much is in flux here as it never takes form as it does in the physical.

I take great pleasure at watching the ease with which you can create and mold and change in this the astral space. It is impressive indeed - how you come here with little effort and how you return. It is not a surprise that you feel trapped in some way upon that return, for I would feel the same. I think you sense the truth behind it all though, so as we proceed, let me send these words to you down a lovely slide, or a cascading waterfall, or a slippery slide at an amusement park, or a green and grassy hillside in spring. I will roll the words down to you and you will gracefully pick them up, because you flow there as my receiver, as you flow when you are there on the summit. I am witness to much here, but see little that compares to what you are able to achieve in spite of your doubts and fears. I applaud your perseverance.

O T H E R S

I could spend much time telling you about the others who are here with me. There are many who would be familiar to you. The first to come to mind, the brightest light I ever wanted and loved to see as I passed, that darling boy who walked through the light, his arms outstretched to me, his uncle, his brother, his friend, Henry. Waldo's boy, the dearest of children was there to greet me. How precious he had been in life and how precious here, taking my hand as I had so many times taken his. He helped to cross me over into this place.

You have written sweet images of my brother and me. I cherish those moments in your story for they capture the feelings that we had then.[32] I cry still to think of the loss we suffered, but of course when passing we were reunited and I could then see the larger plan at play. I do not wish to regret any days of my life, but I regret those that I lost in grief to this man who now stands beside me again. We must continue on our journey always in life and know that we will reunite again at some point with those who pass

---

[32] He refers to scenes in my book, *Honor in Concord*, that involve Thoreau and his brother, John.

before us, and that in fact those who pass before do not ever leave us. That was and will always be so.

There are bands of love, groups who collect in similarity and sympathy, who hold together as glue as we relate and work together on a shared cause. You are one with this group of us divine light souls and that is why this interaction occurs and why those here want to help and assist to bring this book that speaks of truth in spirit to light.

If you lift your energies to our level and we combine our efforts we will produce a wonderful gift for the world, a true treasure, for the truest treasures bring about transformation of the soul. Transformation and fulfillment comes through revelation, knowledge, wisdom and love. Dust off your old thoughts and reach for the sky. Lift up your spirit and allow yourself to grow and change and come out of the place that holds you and brings you down.

L O U I S A

There are many here who would wish to speak to you and through you. There is one, Louisa[33], who sees in you the same fierceness as in she, this desire to stand on your own feet and not live as other women do in the shadows of their men. She gained this strength from her mother, who too was a strong woman and remains so here, but it is Louisa who wants to speak now.

Cathryn, you are stronger, or at least more defiant in your nature than me in wanting to be even freer than me, for that is something I could not be. My family they were to me my rock, my place in this world. I may not have anchored to a man, but I anchored to my family, to my mother and to my father. It is difficult to explain my life to many, but perhaps not to you who sustains a similar form of focus on herself and her work. I do admire your freedom but not the lonely times that you spend. I did not have the physical aspects of love that women do and you in your day and

---

[33] Louisa May Alcott (1832-1888) - Author of *Little Women*.

mores have been allowed those experiences and that has changed your view. I do witness this pain in you and the loneliness may be greater as a result. I did not know what I was missing, is what I am saying to you. I laugh here. That is my joke. I know more now, but I did know of love and related so to your love for the dark one. You have an intensity in the emotions and I had that, too. Alas, these are difficult subjects to address, one of myself to one such as you in your time. I feel demure in a sense, laughing again. I am talking as girlfriends talk, as I would talk to my sisters, broken and strange and full of laughing and innuendo of such things we should never speak of and then we laugh more. You understand how sisters speak. Will you write a book for and about me?

But first things first, there is Henry; the dearest friend, the most mysterious and rough and humble of father's friends. He was like a boy to us, with his visits. We related to him as one of the boys we knew and wanted more to play with him, for that is how Henry was with the children, always wanting to connect to their laughter and joy and the connection to spirit that they still had that the adults seemed not to. His passing was heartbreak to us all, and I pondered on it for many years. It was a great joy to me to find him here with father when I arrived. And so many here! All who you love, all who have lived are here, but you know that! Oh, I would like to continue, but I will let Henry return now. Stay strong and persevere and know we are here as friends and family to you and as spirits who connect and resonate as you do. We will speak again.

* * *

Louisa is a joy to me here. I am forever delighted in her company. There is so much excitement in her about all of this, but you will need to stay in balance, and this issue of whether it is real or not is one you will have to reconcile. I cannot explain any more than to say, what is real anyway? Reality is something that we take part in creating. In the physical world it is more tangible, more relatable. In our world reality is always shifting and changing. It is like a million plays going on at the same time and the writer there with his eraser, writing and rewriting the scene. Let's play it this way, let's play it that way. At the end of the scene every fallen body, every broken heart, every sprain or scrape or scar or tangle, is all untangled, unbroken, and most importantly undead, and we all get up and do it again. Why? To learn. That is the simplest explanation. And when there is less left to learn there is less need for incarnation, for being a player in the play, and sometimes well...we just vacation.

EMERSON

Let me see if anyone else will come forth today. I see Waldo. He stands up and it is as if he is 30 feet tall. He continues to tower over the rest of us, as he did in life. This strange tall wise soul, what a monument he is to purity and truth. I admire him for that. You get a humble bow and wave from him today, but nothing more. I am not sure who else will share their words.

CYNTHIA DUNBAR THOREAU

My mother, ha, she will share words with everyone. She is here at last, delay, delay. It took her a while to arrive. She is here now, bothering at me. I am telling her no she must not take part. She sends her love anyway, thanking you for your regard for me and the others, and then she drifts away.

MARGARET FULLER

I wish I could say that Margaret was here now to speak to you, as I can tell it is what you would wish but she is not here or ready to proceed in such manner. She was brilliant. We all knew that, although some could not allow her the full experience of her wisdom because she was after all a woman. I laugh at that sentiment. How foolish men can be who refuse to acknowledge the brilliance that equals or betters their own, simply because it comes in the form of female. The wisdom at the source of each of us is the same, and comes from the shared spirit, not from the body. Again, the misplaced understanding. We think we are our bodies and we are not.

There is a vast difference between the life that is lived there and the existence we have here in spirit. As one who can perceive both, you can appreciate that distinction.

There is a man in the distance, someone else who wishes to speak to you. He is such a talker though, you must be warned, that he will not cease once he has begun. Are you certain you are ready for this?

AMOS BRONSON ALCOTT

What is this we have here? Who is this woman who possesses such a gift as this? Do not fear me, for I am not a gray bearded marauder, I am simply myself, this farmer, this philosopher, this Holy Spirit. Let me speak then as I will now speak to you for that is what I am best known for. Laughing if you will, it is okay, for many laughed at me and my ideas, but my ideas continue and linger in spite of those who would not have paid me a nickel for my thoughts. Listen now as I tell you with utter truth in my voice that the spirits that surround you and love and protect you do so with great good and desire to assist and you must never fall short of your service to them. I wish to congratulate you in this endeavor, as others have, too, for it is a mysterious and incredible one, to be sure. I will not linger too long as I have much more work to be done here. You can find me in the fields out near Fruitlands. That was my utopia, that beautiful place. I wander through still from time to time, and think back on how wonderful it was and on how difficult it was.

I do not think it is easy for one such as me, and such as you may be at times, who have such an ideal of purpose and perfection and who desire to see the world in a certain way, rather than to confront the essentials of life as Henry put it, the roughness and meanness of it. We do not like to linger in the muck and the mire, but instead to linger in our thoughts of other realms where such things as hillsides and sunshine and blue skies and the growth and the beauty of earth are there and can in an instant transform into another vision of a place where we might rather be. It is effortless transformation on this side whereas everything in the physical realm requires great effort and concentration. I do not have to tell you how difficult it is to transform one's self, and I found it equally difficult. There is not much of physical life that did not cause me to stop and reconsider it at any given time. I struggled every day and if not for the enterprising daughter I bred, or the industrious wife I so fortuitously fell in love with, then I would not have survived for as long as I did, for I longed for the level of transformation that I found here, and I had instead the roadblocks that I often felt there, and that is something that you and I share.

I do not wish to pretend a familiarity with you beyond this first introduction. We did know each other in other times and places but you are not so familiar with those times so I will not be either. Listen to my words as I say that I am he who speaks to you this day and remembers then. I will be here on this hillside, looking out at the glorious Wachusett[34] and we will speak again when there is more time for I would also like to partake in what may be something remarkable.

I remember a time when there was great joy in the streets of the village of Concord and when I walked through in long coat and tall hat and my daughters walked with me and we stood among the people there who admired us well and recognized our worth. Welcome to the eternity of me and of all of us here who care.

After the departure of Bronson Alcott, my connection began to weaken again so with the following words from Thoreau we were done for the day.

DISTANT AND FAR FROM CONCORD

Distant and far from Concord is the place I now dwell. Here it is as if you could be and are anyone you wish to be. Here there are instant rewards and instant punishments. Here there exists the possibility for all. So, with thought we drift to the places that are most important to us and in those moments we are what we most

---

[34] Reference to Wachusett Mountain which is clearly seen from the hillside where the home Bronson Alcott called "Fruitlands" still stands in Harvard, Massachusetts.

wish ourselves to be. For me this will always and forever be a quiet place with scenic views far from the crowds of city life and far from the thoughts of others who do interfere with our own.

Find for yourself a quiet place where you can reach in and explore the depths of yourself. You may find it only in your bed at night or in a small room or corner of your home and for a short time each day when only you are there, take the time to quiet your mind and to listen. For you must do that, we must all do that, if we are to understand who we are and who we can be.

HUMBLE RECOGNITION

Lift up your glass then, whether real or imagined, in tribute to this divinely inspired and true cause. It is not our purpose to elevate ourselves any further because for some there is not much further we could go in elevation. How well we are regarded by many, how much we are treasured. We are humbled by this, because as I have said to you in prior communications, we are merely messengers of a more divine message and it is the message that must be praised and not the man or woman who sends it.

Come and dance and sing and play, and look not into the darkness and the darkest of man's expressions as if they are more real and true than those that come from the light. Direct yourself toward the higher vibrations and more true knowledge will come to you. There are no walls to meet in expanding your knowledge. There is no limit to the totality of who you are.

I am in a high mode, yes, excited to reach in and play with this mind that controls these fingers that glide over the keys of this machine that records. What I would not have done in my day to possess such a machine as this!

***

Chapter Twenty-two
UFOs

"There were in my time those who reported objects in flight in our skies."

The subject of extraterrestrials is one that for many is sheer fantasy but to me they are fact. I am one of the many people who are considered "experiencers" by those who research the alien abduction phenomenon and for a short time beginning in 2007 I was a member of a group of experiencers that take their strength and identity from the group's original founder, Harvard Medical School professor and renounced alien abduction researcher, Dr. John Mack.

Dr. Mack was a well respected professor of psychology at Harvard University in Cambridge, Massachusetts. He won a Pulitzer Prize in 1977 for the biography he wrote about T.E. Lawrence, the English man best known as Lawrence of Arabia, but when his book *Abductions* was published in 1994, and the extensive research he had done into the alien abduction phenomenon was revealed, his life was forever changed. Harvard University feared the negative impact that his research would have on the University, and his credibility was challenged by the media and the public, but his research had made Dr. Mack a true believer and he continued to be an outspoken advocate for many like me who have personally experienced this phenomenon. He was greatly admired and is considered a hero by many of us and, whether or not we had known him personally, the news of his tragic death in London on September 27, 2004 was devastating. Dr. Mack was hit and killed by a drunk driver while walking on a London street after delivering a speech to a gathering of the T.E. Lawrence Society. There has been speculation about a conspiracy to end his life and his research, but his death is accepted by most to have been accidental.

It was in 2007, three years after Dr. Mack's death, and while in the midst of channeling Thoreau, when I joined a group of experiencers that included many of the original members of the group Dr. Mack had formed in Cambridge in the 1990s. Many of them are accomplished individuals, and I felt privileged to become a part of their group, but due to some philosophical differences, I remained a member for only a short time.

On Sunday, June 1, 2008, a meeting of this group was held at the townhouse where I was living then in Bedford, and where the channeling of this book was at that time actively taking place. I had warned in advance that it was a small space for such a large group to gather and we would be crowded together, but all were willing to endure the inconvenience. The day before the meeting, while I went about setting up the small living room with every chair that I had in the place, I chatted away with Brad and Henry, and felt confident that they heard me. This wasn't unusual. I often chatted away at them and there were many times when Rev. Barbara, or other psychics I had readings with, would repeat back to me the exact questions I had asked them during such times and then give me their answers to those questions. That day, amid the chatter that involved all kinds of apprehension on my part about so many people being in the space that had become so sacred to me, I extended an invitation to Henry that he should feel free to join us the next day for the meeting. Brad's invitation was not as direct. To me it was just a given that Brad would be there because in those days it seemed he was always there with me. Then as my thoughts turned to worry over whether or not there would be enough coffee and food on hand, I forgot all about having invited Henry.

We were about half way through the meeting the following afternoon when I began to sense something was there in the small space between the large living room chair where I was seated and the television that was on the table maybe two feet away. I turned my head to look a couple of times but I didn't see anything exactly – at least not in any usual sense of that word - but before I could put two and two together and figure out who or what it was that I was seeing one of the other members asked, *"What does Thoreau look like?"* When I showed her his picture that I kept in a frame on my bookshelf she smiled and then pointed to that place near the television that had drawn my attention and calmly informed the group, *"He is standing right there."* Immediately I knew she was right. Having chosen to accept the invitation I had extended to him, Thoreau was there, standing next to the chair where I was seated, listening to the conversation and enjoying everything that was taking place.

I had revealed to the group the first time I met with them the nature of the communication I was engaged in with Thoreau. It was easy to share such information with people who had experiences of their own that stretched the boundary of believability and lived day-to-day, as I did, with an expanded sense of what was real and possible. They had no trouble accepting my claim of communication with the supposedly long dead Thoreau. They were delighted to learn he had joined us and they urged me to share with them whatever it was that he had to say.

It was not the best of circumstances for me to relay a message from him, feeling as uncomfortable as I did with nine pairs of eyes focused on me, but I went ahead and tried to connect anyway. The first thing I was able to pick up from him was the absolute joy he was feeling at being there. The way we had gathered together to share and discuss our own experiences and ideas was very much like he and his friends would do in their day. He enjoyed the relaxed and casual atmosphere and the level of intelligence of this group that was quite high. As I focused in though I realized that Thoreau was concerned, much as I had always been but hadn't yet found a way to express, about the willingness of the group members to accept what the ETs were telling them was factual and true and intended for their benefit. Many members seemed to regard the ETs as superior to us not only in intelligence but as spiritually enlightened beings. They were willing, in some cases, to offer all that they had in exchange for a chance at what they perceived as immortality or for a place of prominence in another world that they were often told was being constructed for them. This kind of blind faith had always made me uncomfortable and was the primary reason I later broke from the group, but at the time of that meeting I had not yet discovered the books by Marshall Vian Summers[35], that would address these concerns so directly, and I had not yet found the courage to express my own such reservations to the group.

When Thoreau's message was a succinct, *"Don't believe everything you hear"* followed by *"Trust the knowledge that is there within you,"* I delivered it reluctantly, knowing that it would not be enough for them, but it seemed more than fitting to me considering the subject that had been presented for discussion that day. One of the group members revealed that they had been receiving specific scientific information from the ETs and, together with one of the most learned members of the group, they were endeavoring to verify this information and felt that the implications, if true, would impact our current understanding of life on this planet. I remained skeptical. It seemed to me that such revelations, if they be true, would only set us up for obligation and dependency upon a race of ETs that I felt certain we could not trust, and it appeared that Thoreau agreed with me.

It was a few months later when I discovered a book called, *Allies of Humanity* by Marshall Vian Summers. Summers, who is an admirer of Thoreau, claims his books contain material channeled directly from a group of ETs whose intent is to fight against what he considers the predatory race of ETs who are influencing the overall consciousness of this planet. His book, *Allies of Humanity* contains what he calls *"an urgent message about the alien presence in the world today"*, and speaks to what is to me the largest concern of our time - the inability to see clearly through the idealism and the falsity that dominates our present culture.

In the fall of 2008, we had not yet reached the date, December 28, 2012. It was the date that was supposed to mark an energetic shift for the world and had been considered by some as a possible end of times as it coincided with the end of the Mayan

---

[35] I first read, *Allies of Humanity*, by Marshall Vian Summers' in August of 2008, two months after the meeting of experiencers at my home in Bedford.

Calendar in apocalyptic predictions from many sources throughout the world. As much as I see the awakening that is taking place, I still see the masses of men who Thoreau described as *"leading lives of quiet desperation"*. I believe that is because of a lack of understanding of their true spiritual natures. They deny the reality of spirit each day by their actions and interactions with each other. They are unaware that every thought, every deed, every action they take matters.

A short time after he had appeared during the gathering of experiencers at my place in Bedford, I received the following transmissions from Thoreau on the subject of UFOs:

OBJECTS IN FLIGHT IN OUR SKIES

There were in my time those who reported objects in flight in our skies. Of course then there would have been no explanation for how such a thing could be, other than a large bird that might have the capacity to take flight. There were no motorized vehicles that could soar to the heights so when things were reported it was a mystery to all as to how one who seemed so rational and calm, so real as any of the rest of us, could imagine such an object in the sky. I fear that many were ridiculed as they are still today when forced to confess such a sighting and that many found that their lives had been changed as a result. It is an act of unkindness to dismiss those who report such things rather than weighing instead their common bond of truth.

What appeals to me most in the revelations that come from such a sighting is that there is more and perhaps it sets the sighted one to inner reflection and puts an emphasis on discovering more about life and self through that reflection. I did this myself in my own life as I saw things that proved to me the validity of life in this universe. We who gathered in my time would occasionally engage in speculation about such things. We were not without imagination after all. We did not regularly imagine such things as what are now commonplace, like the jet airplane or the television and radio, but

177

we did at times imagine what it would be like if there was life on a world in a distant universe. We did not call them aliens, ETs or UFOs, but we would occasional speak of star people. That was something we might consider with humor and then let the idea slide for none of us was ready to harvest that concept. We had not yet seen airplanes, only birds could fly so high, and to imagine a world of so much more was an unusual thing indeed.

I am now, from this perspective able to see and understand the vastness of this universe and recognize our profound place in it. If you understand that there are others out there then you must be prepared to defend yourself against them. You must be prepared to fight to preserve your own freedom and not become subjects to them because of their mastery of technology. You must instead demand their respect and meet them as equals who inhabit a universe.

It is the desire of one life form to dominate another that is the basis for all evil in the system of life. As humans you are the occupants and should be the preservationists of this planet.

THE ALIEN PRESENCE

There is such a complex matrix of ideas and personalities in the universe. You cannot imagine the depth of thoughts and range of thoughts that exist and all of them influence reality.

The nature of the universe is not an all loving one it is a competitive one as all races must fight for the things that sustain their own lives. There are different awarenesses within these individual societies as well, so one race of aliens may not be aware of spirit in any way and act and interact as if there is no spiritual level. Others are well aware and because of that they act in ways that are more respectful and do not come and attempt to impede or impair our lives.

PLACES OF TOTAL DARKNESS

Do not think that there will be any rewards offered by those who wish to snatch us up and transport us to their worlds. There are places of total darkness in this universe where there is limited or no spiritual awareness at all and in those worlds we would be relegated to the lowest position in the hierarchy. In those worlds they live in a way that denies the reality of God, but they will also see and confront eternity when they pass from their physical forms just as we do.

REALITY OF SPIRIT

Do not deny the reality of spirit or the importance of being tied in strongly to your own knowledge because that is where you will find the strength that you need to get you through the most difficult times. It matters not whether you find this strength through Christian, Muslim, or Buddhist practices, it matters only that you find it for it is the bond itself and not the traditions that matter. In its highest form it is there for you as a resource for truth and wisdom and if you follow the guidance it provides for you then you will yourself see the risks that are inherent in seeking out Gods from other alien cultures. They are not Gods. In many cases they are not nearly as wise or aware as yourselves.

* * *

"Perchance, coming generations will not abide the dissolution of the globe, but, availing themselves of future inventions in aerial locomotion, and the navigation of space, the entire race may migrate from the earth, to settle some vacant and more western planet.... "
- Henry David Thoreau, Paradise Regained (1842)

"As we looked up in silence to those distant lights, we were reminded that it was a rare imagination which first taught that the stars are worlds, and had conferred a great benefit on mankind."
-Henry David Thoreau, A Week On the Concord and Merrimack Rivers (1849)

"In our science and philosophy, even, there is commonly no true and absolute account of things. The spirit of sect and bigotry has planted its hoof amid the stars. You have only to discuss the problem, whether the stars are inhabited or not, in order to discover it."
- Henry David Thoreau, Life Without Principle (1863)

Chapter Twenty-three
Touring Thoreau's Worcester

...and I knew that meant he had found Henry there, too.

My book, *Honor in Concord*, was published in July 2008, just in time for me to carry one copy to the annual gathering that year and play show and tell with it during the book signing that is always reserved for presenters at the gathering, but which I was allowed to crash. It was fun and a great feeling to have that book in my hands at last, but I realized soon after that the reality of self-publishing was that in addition to all the costs involved, all of the work involved in promoting the book would also fall on me. It was daunting to say the least. One of the first things I did was to call the local newspaper, The Concord Journal, and ask if they might be interested in interviewing me, a local author with a newly published book about Concord. The next thing I knew there was a photographer at my door in Bedford, wanting to photograph me there with the book and also positioned near Thoreau's grave on Author's Ridge at Sleepy Hollow.

The interview that was to be published with those pictures was to take place late afternoon on September 5, 2008, the same day I had previously scheduled my long-awaited tour of Thoreau's Worcester with Thoreauvian, Edmond A. Schofield. Ed, who was a professor at Worcester Polytechnic for many years, was one of the senior members of the Thoreau Society. He had been a frequenter of Concord long before my first arrival there, and although we had often seen and acknowledged each other at the annual gatherings and

some other local events, over the years, we never really had a chance
to talk or get to know each other until I won the bid and purchased
this tour from the Thoreau Society's fundraising auction the previous
fall. Because of some changes in Ed's life it had taken nearly a year
for us to determine a date for the tour so once we did I wasn't about
to reschedule it.

Ed had grown up in Worcester, Massachusetts and he loved
it, in spite of its current reputation as a rough and rugged city with a
high rate of crime. Ed knew Worcester's history, he loved its
architecture, its parks, and the strength of its past, and he was writing
a book about it that he was excited to talk about as our tour began.
My own book had been out for two months at that point, and I told
Ed about it that day, but I never mentioned the other aspect of my
work that I expected he would never be able to understand or relate
to. Even when Ed casually mentioned to me that he had once given
this tour to Brad and his wife, I said nothing. I mean what was I
going to say?

I drove out to Worcester that morning and picked Ed up at
the place he had indicated, alongside one of the streets downtown,
and then we headed over to the historical society to begin what
turned out to be a delightful day, visiting all of the places in
Worcester that Thoreau was known to have frequented or that had
some significance to him. Among those places was Mechanic's
Hall, a concert hall built in 1857, where Thoreau had once lectured.
Ed and I were both excited to see the actual podium from which
Thoreau, on November 3, 1859, had delivered his impassioned *Plea
for Captain John Brown*, and from which other notables, including
Emerson had also lectured. After that we went to the records room
at the courthouse building, where we examined legal documents
having to do with Worcester native, H.G.O. Blake's inheritance of
Thoreau's manuscripts, per the terms of his sister, Sophia Thoreau's
will. We also did silly things like climb the stairs at the rear of the
bank building downtown because Ed believed Thoreau had once
climbed them and more serious things, like going to the mayor's
office at City Hall because Ed wanted to introduce me to the mayor,
who he was evidently already acquainted with. Unfortunately for
me, the mayor was unavailable, so we spent some time admiring the

old City Hall building instead. It was built after Thoreau's death so did not offer a Thoreauvian connection per se, but it was on the National Register of Historic Buildings and deemed worthy of consideration.

Ed was enthusiastic but cautious with me at first that day. He was unsure if he should let on how excited he was to be at these places where Thoreau had once been, no matter how many times he had been there before. He seemed to relax though, after I assured him that I was just as excited to be there as he was. I was at least that much of a true Thoreauvian myself and Ed, realizing this, and recognizing that the anxiety that I felt in social settings was the reason for the silence I often displayed when he had seen me at the Thoreau Society gatherings in the past, began to get over his own shyness towards me. Halfway through the day he began calling me "Dear Heart". I was Ed's dear heart that day and it was the sweetest thing to hear him call me that.

Of all the places we visited during our tour my favorite was the photography studio in downtown Worcester that was once known as Benjamin D. Maxham's studio. Thoreau went there June 18, 1856 to have his photograph taken and although it was 150 yrs later and the studio was now under another name, Ed and I were there to be in that same space where Thoreau had once been photographed. Ed was friendly with the owners and he had alerted them ahead of time of our visit, so they had set up a display showing copies of the three Maxham daguerreotype images of Thoreau that were taken there in 1856. They were also prepared and insistent that they take a photograph of Ed and I, with me holding a photo of Thoreau, to commemorate the occasion, but I was reluctant. I am perpetually camera shy, and was feeling overheated and fatigued from running around Worcester on one of the hottest days that summer, but after my initial protests I did finally agree and the photograph was taken. I was insistent though that I not see the photo. I did not want a bad picture of myself to spoil for me what had been a very enjoyable day.

The tour ended in the same place it had begun, back at the small parking lot near the historical society where I had left my car. I gave Ed a copy of my book, *Honor in Concord*, and he seemed happy to receive it and genuinely excited about reading it, and I hoped he would enjoy it even if it wasn't exactly the academic fair he was used to consuming. Then, just as we were saying our good-byes a puff of smoke rose up out of one of the homes a few streets over and that meant Ed had to go. He tucked the book under his arm, thanked me and then took off at a slow jog running in the direction of the apparent house fire, and I got into my car and headed back to my place in Bedford, hoping I would get there in time to clean up a bit before my interview at The Concord Journal.

Ed emailed me later that night, several times, until he got my reply. He was just making sure I got home okay and he seemed relieved to know that I had, but I never saw Ed again after that day of our tour of Worcester in September 2008. The interview at The Concord Journal did not go that well. Exhausted from my day running around Worcester in over 90 degree heat and more than a little nervous, my speech was broken and nonsensical and there would be no corrections or changes made to the copy of the interview transcript that I was allowed to see prior to publication, no matter how hard I pleaded with the young reporter to make them. Besides the broken speech, I had revealed to him the Thoreau phenomenon I was involved in and this did nothing but set the pace for a strange article that left me feeling humiliated and kept me hiding out in my house and shopping for groceries in adjacent communities for weeks to come. I did not want to run into anyone who might recognize me and I did not want to face anyone from the Thoreau Society who might question what I had said.

And perhaps it was that article that Ed had told me he would look for, or perhaps it was in response to my book that he had told me he would read, but Ed never contacted me again and I did not have the courage or the confidence to contact him, and when the annual gathering came around the following July I was not there for it. I had moved from Bedford back into Concord in July 2009 and came down with a cold that kept me from attending the annual gathering that year. So when the email arrived in April 2010, informing all Thoreau Society members that Ed had been found dead at the train station in his beloved Worcester, I simply couldn't believe another of the key figures in my Thoreauvian world had passed so suddenly.

I hadn't wanted to see the photo that was taken of Ed and me that day in Worcester, in what had been Maxham's studio, so they had promised to send a copy to Ed, but I never received one and never saw the photo until I walked into the United Congregational Church in Worcester where the memorial service for Ed was held. There we were, Ed and I, blown up to poster size and displayed for all to see as they came into his service. Ed looks glowing and happy in the photo and I look frazzled from the heat but otherwise okay, and there in my hands is the photo of Henry that they asked me to hold up for the camera.

I never told Ed during our tour that day that I was involved in this phenomenon with Thoreau, but once Ed passed, I knew he had been completely informed. There was only one occasion when I felt I connected to Ed after his death, and it was when he came through briefly to confirm that he had in fact found his friend, Brad there, and I knew that meant he had found Henry there, too.

* * *

Chapter Twenty-four
A TRIP TO WASHINGTON D.C.

"We are entitled to the fruits of our own labors."

On September 11, 2008, three and a half years after my mother's passing, two months after my book, *Honor in Concord* was published and the very day that the article about me and my book appeared in both local newspapers, The Concord Journal and The Bedford Minuteman, I drove to Washington, D.C. to attend the brief internment ceremony that placed my mother's ashes along with my father's at Arlington National Cemetery. I was relieved to be getting out of town that day since I considered that article to be a complete disaster and preferred to be nowhere to be seen or recognized as long as my photo and the story about me were on the front page of both the local newspapers.

My mother had passed three years earlier, so the mood of our family gathering was not as mournful as it might otherwise have been for such an occasion. In fact, my sisters and I, who each lived in different states, viewed this as a rare opportunity to spend some time together and high on our list of things to do while in D.C. was to tour President Lincoln's Cottage on the Soldier's Home property on the northwest side of the city. It is said to have been a sanctuary for the Lincolns during Lincoln's presidency and had recently been restored and opened to the public. As beautiful as the landscaping and the buildings appeared, both the Lincoln Cottage and the Soldier's Home itself (now known and functioning as the Armed Forces Retirement Home), there was an ominous feeling about the place that I sensed from the minute we arrived. The pain and the anguish that was the reality of the times they lived in had never fully dissipated, and the photos on display in the visitor's center confirmed this for me and only increased the sense I had of the loss, pain and suffering that had been endured there.

I know a man who is both a shaman and a psychic, who once told me that he believed the spirit of President Lincoln had never crossed over. He said he had been looking for him for many years but hadn't yet found him. As I stepped into the cottage that was once Lincoln's home I wondered if I might find Lincoln there, but it was a large crowd who gathered for the tour that day, and I was too distracted by all the people around me, including my sisters, to be able to focus in any way on the energies in the home. That was true at first anyway, but when we set foot in the living room and the tour guide began to speak in particular about Lincoln's emancipation proclamation I felt my energies suddenly shift. Well, it is more accurate to say, I felt them shifted for me and I knew I was to pay close attention to what the tour guide was preparing to say.

He was talking about the time Lincoln had spent in this home writing the emancipation proclamation - the document that contained Lincoln's directive to free the slaves - and as he spoke I received a download of information and experienced the most profound sense of déjà vu that I have ever felt. I suddenly knew that I had been in that house before and I remembered seeing Lincoln there with me, not as the unsettled ghostly spirit that my friend believed him to be, but as the man he was in that home during his lifetime.

This was a surprising revelation to say the least. I often speculated about past lives I might have had in Concord and Cambridge, and have had psychics tell me the same, but in that moment at the Lincoln's summer home I flashed back on a past life that had once brought me there. And, while I stood there among the crowd of people on the tour and with my sisters from this life at my side, it was also revealed to me that Thoreau had been there at that time, too, but not in physical form. I was told that upon arriving on the other side, Thoreau recognized the liberty that existed for him there, and knowing that he could from that side influence and assist in whatever way he could for the causes that he had fought for and that had meant so much to him, Thoreau had turned his attention to President Lincoln. He had sought him out and he had found him there at his summer home working on the Emancipation Proclamation.

In that house Lincoln and his wife, Mary Todd Lincoln, often welcomed spiritualists. They had lost a son, Willie, recently, and Mary found comfort in the words of spiritualists who would assure her that Willie was safe and alive on the other side. But there was more to the spiritualist connection with the Lincolns, for not only were they connecting with beloved family and friends, they were connecting with others in spirit who were doing what they could to aid Lincoln as he prepared this most important historic document. I was told that Thoreau was one of those spirits. Thoreau had not lived to see freedom for the slaves, but he had aided in bringing it about in this most extraordinary way.

This was a fantastic revelation to me as I received it, as I am sure it is for many as they read it here, but does it not make sense that once free Thoreau would choose to travel, as he did, to the place where he would find the man who held the most power to change this great wrong that Thoreau himself had fought against? Would he not, given the opportunity, aid and assist Lincoln, in whatever way possible, in the preparation of the document that would bring freedom to so many?

Of this and of Lincoln, I was later told by Thoreau:

PROMISE OF FREEDOM

Of course I would hold to me this promise of freedom. I would do what I was able to do to assist this tired and worn and deeply troubled man. He was not as great and strong a man as some figured. He was determined though and he played a role that was set out for him. He played it well and he succeeded in the end to achieve the goals that so many of us who lived then had fought for. Lincoln's thoughts were influenced as he sought reconciliation between all the conflicting ideas of his time. He did ultimately what was right, and he bore out the truest concession that all are created equal and all have a right to their personal sovereignty. This was his greatest mission and accomplishment. This was his truest gem. But Lincoln was not a free man or soul and I still worry for the place that he was left in. There was no time for relief and revelation, or for understanding that what he had accomplished was great and that he would be remembered well. The man who shot him took this from him and left him with a blow that would take centuries to heal.

There were two key points that were emphasized to me about this revelation. The first was that not only were the slaves freed by the emancipation proclamation, but that all men, regardless of what role they had played in this abomination, had been freed. Because, whether or not an action is taken for or against our will, any action of domination or submission has a karmic impact on both parties.

The other point Thoreau emphasized at this time in the transmissions and through downloads of information to me was his belief that all men are entitled to the fruits of their own labors so therefore any thought of "spreading the wealth" as was being talked about in the media so much at that time was fundamentally wrong. It was, in Thoreau's view, just another kind of slavery, the kind where we work as slaves to the government.

Of this he said:

THE INDIVIDUAL MAN

Each man must take responsibility for his own life. He must seek to find ways to appease his hunger, warm his cold, feed his children. It is a part of the lesson of life on this planet that we must seek and find and thrive individually before we can take those rewards to the whole. If the rewards are given out, the prizes are received before the battle is won, then why fight the battle? Why play the game? The steps on the way to the truth are as valuable as the truth itself. The steps we take on the road to divinity are important to knowing it and recognizing it when we see it.

Think then of the highest heights of the mountain and those who stand below it as meager, small souls, who want so much to venture up. They must climb each step, seek and find their shelter, seek and find the solid place for their foot to rest. Would not their victory be less victorious as they reached the apex, if they had been assisted at each point along the way, if there had been a comfortable wrap provided, a full meal waiting, had they been given a map so that each step they took could be received well and solidly?

The victories in life are hard won. True learning comes to the individual who advances on their own path. We are not meant to be appeased, or eased, we are meant to lift ourselves up and to learn on our own.

In this day and age when we hear words spoken about a need to share our profits and spread the wealth, Thoreau is reminding us of the fundamental principles that guaranty freedom for each man, sovereignty of the individual and the rights to the fruits of our own labors. That is the view he takes. If a man chooses to keep the fruits of his own labors to himself, so be it. It is his right, but a more conscious man will see things in a proper perspective. He will know what it is he must do to create the best circumstance for all and he will gladly share the bounty.

Around this time the words "Conscious Capitalism" came to me to describe what Thoreau was outlining as the preferred and proper economic principle. Just as he wanted a government made up of people with a conscience, he relies upon the conscience of the individual to know when it is proper to share in the bounty each individual creates. To take from any man the fruits of his labor is to deny him his fundamental right and impose upon him a type of slavery that Thoreau had spoken out against all his life. It is a matter of conscience and responsibility of the individual. No man can force another to share what is rightfully his without falling into a pattern of thievery or slavery. That is how Thoreau saw it then and now.

Freedom does not come when a government dictates to you what you must do with what is rightfully yours. With a proper conscience and connection to source, a man will always know and will always choose to share his bounty and that is to Thoreau another example of right action.

THE FRUITS OF OUR LABORS

We are entitled to the fruits of our own labors. That is a fundamental principle and one that must be heeded. Without it we become slaves again, if not slavery from man to man, it is slavery from man to his government.

The government treats its citizens as slaves when it demands the money a man earns and then does what it wants with that money. No government has the right to take a man's money. No man has that right either.

A BETTER INDIVIDUAL

You ask then how do we provide for the underprivileged, for those in society who society wrecks? How will we care for the other? This we will do through conscience. Just as I asked for a better government, I ask for a better individual. I would ask for the strength and wisdom of the individual to know within him that he must reach out and assist his fellow man and he will do that. We see it played out all the time in situations when we come upon danger or hazard. Nine times out of ten the individuals who are there will try to save the one who is harmed. It is human nature to do this, it is the nature of the divine and those who have a connection with the divine will act accordingly.

In the case of providing for others in a day-to-day sense, we need only rely on the wisdom within each of us to know that this must be done and to know when it should be done and when we are awakened to the truth of our own natures and continued existence, then we will act accordingly. We will take care of each other. And yet maintain our right to free enterprise, to reap the rewards from our own labors and to choose what to do with those rewards.

A   W I S E   W O R L D

In a wise world of conscious individuals we will give freely and wisely and all will benefit. In a conscious society we do not need the hard whip of the master in the form of government, to insist that our money be shared. Why not a system where each individual may give as much or as little as they desire to any cause that they chose? It will be a freer world and a more intelligent, and compassionate world. In that system we are no longer children, doing as we are told by the government master, we are acting from a place of true connection and true wisdom and doing what we know to be right. That is the distinction. That is the proper way.

* * *

Chapter Twenty-five
The Chain-Link Fence

"Understand that the universe is complex and creative, above all else it is creative."

On September 16, 2008, I was interviewed for The Commonwealth Journal, a program broadcast on WUMB - the radio station of the University of Massachusetts in Boston. The interview would not air until nearly a month later, but the following day I found myself feeling distraught over my inability when interviewed to express in a clear way what it was that I was experiencing, and in doubt once again over the reality of what was occurring. Then, seemingly in response to this dark and doubt-filled mood I had allowed myself to drop into, I received a transmission about, of all things, a chain-link fence.

At the time I received this transmission, I had no idea where or when the first chain-link fence was invented or when it was first made in the United States. I have since researched and learned the following: The firm of Barnard, Bishop & Barnard was established in Norwich in the United Kingdom to produce chain-link fencing by machine. The process was developed by Charles Barnard in 1844 based on cloth weaving machines. Anchor Fence (established in 1891) was the first company in the United States to manufacture chain-link fencing by machines using equipment imported from Belgium. That was 29 years after Thoreau's death.

THE CHAIN-LINK FENCE

There is a chain-link fence a short distance from where you live. I look at it often and wonder at how such a device has been created and born and exists now in the way that it does. In my day we did not have this item, and yet it seems **a** simple concept to everyone now as we look at it and see how each of the links come together. I want to use this fence now as a symbol of two things. First, it exists now as something that did not exist then and was not thought about or known about and when discovered was thought to be extraordinary or new, and yet the materials for that fence had been there all along. That is how you must now think about this process of spirit that you are experiencing and that you will reveal to the public, one link at a time.

Understand that the universe is complex and creative, above all else it is creative. We usher in a new link to our fence with each thought that we have, and there are those of us who are bound together by shared thought or philosophy. Through our shared knowledge we are one, and you are one with all of us who share that chain-link fence. Know that to be true and you will then feel better.

The chain-link fence, with its interlocking links that hold together and create this boundary, this strength, is symbolic for the souls who cast themselves out and then come together to build a force against all resistance.

The next time I left the townhouse in Bedford after receiving that message I went in search of the chain-link fence that had caught Henry's eye. A simple metal chain-link fence is such a common feature of residential America that I was sure there must be many nearby that I had never paid any attention to before and I wasn't sure how I was going to know which one it was that had made such an impression on Thoreau. Then I saw it. It was not the normal silver metal chain-link fence that is so commonly seen it was instead a large oversized black fence that provided an impressive fortress for the relatively modest looking home behind it. It was so impressive in fact that I wondered why it had never caught my eye in the same way before. Surely I must have seen it during the many times I had driven past on my way into Concord but now I looked at it in a new way and, having found and confirmed that there was in fact an impressive chain-link fence not even a mile from my then home, I accepted it as even further confirmation that what I was experiencing was in fact what I believed it to be.

Later, when I returned to my desk, having let go of my doubts once again and with my confidence in the process restored, I was told:

MASTERY

We find you in moments when you are so busy that you are no longer caught up in doubt or fear but are concentrating on the work that you are doing. That is a good thing. Mastery of any subject takes time and focus. Your work is larger than the minor concerns that plague you.

"When we are unhurried and wise, we perceive that only great and worthy things have any permanent and absolute existence, that petty fears and petty pleasures are but the shadow of reality."
- Henry David Thoreau, Walden (1854)

* * *

SNIPPETS

Chapter Twenty-six
Snippets of Wisdom

"I am famished to continue this enlightening saga..."

This chapter includes what Thoreau called his "Snippets of Wisdom" that were received at various times throughout this process and that cover many different topics, but all with the same goal of directing us back to the fundamental truths. Many of these snippets came in after the spring of 2009, when the pace we had kept for nearly three years was slowing down. It was a time of transition for me as I was reluctant to let go of the companionship that both Henry and Brad had provided for me but I guess they had said all that there was to say and were ready for me to take these materials and shape them into some kind of book. It would prove to be a daunting task for me and one that would take a considerably long time.

SNIPPETS OF WISDOM

I am famished to continue this enlightening saga, these snippets of wisdom of the past meets present. That is what this is for me you know, how I look back at the past of who I was then and what I knew and learned as that man and how I changed things, me, Henry Thoreau. You see, they have made me into this enormous figure, this mountainlike beast of epic size and strength and they come to me and want to worship at my feet. I have to laugh at what is to me sheer blasphemy. You do not ever worship at the feet of another man, you worship only the strength and the wisdom and the light that is inside of you.

Ironically, I was not of a major size and not of a major strength of character necessarily. Oh, I suspect I was in some ways more courageous as I spoke out for my beliefs, and because I had the gift of language I was able to go far with it and make something. It is clear that I touched upon truth when I directed them toward the inner silence, toward their own inner knowing. That truth is what attracts and calls to people. It is the home they are longing for. They come to this place where I once stayed and long for the peace that they feel I once had there but it is within the power of each of us to create that place for ourselves and that is what I encourage them to do.

D E A T H

Those who think we die when we die are fools and paupers. Their poverty is in their lack of knowing, in their lack of depth and lack of imagination for it is as if to say that we never lived at all to deny the soul. It is the soul that matters most, not the body or any activity of the body. It is the soul that is long lasting and that takes in and considers all things.

C O N S C I O U S N E S S

Think again about this mystery that is life and death. There is no mystery really. It is one long continuous sweep, this ever present consciousness. We may focus our attention on any piece of the puzzle at any time and see more than what we daily see. Be who you are at the soul level, let that magnificence manifest in the world and you will then be the one you were destined to be.

O P E R A   S I N G E R

If you are an opera singer, and you go and sing each night and that is what you live for, then it must be that the song you sing touches the soul of you and the soul of those who listen for that would then be the value in it. If you sing that song for only the money, if you sing for only the pride that you feel or the honor that you feel is bestowed upon you, then you are no longer at work on something for the soul.

SCHOLARSHIP

Scholarship is not a divine process. It is instead something that limits our understanding. I prefer revelation, divine revelation and the flow of truth and it does not require scholarship to be felt and known.

LAUGHTER

Laughter never hurts anyone and always helps to open the channels for what will later flow. You see it is there as a device for greater attunement. If we allow ourselves to atrophy into any particular thought then we have closed out all the frequencies that buzz about around us. That is not a good thing to do.

PRIVACY

We can listen to your thoughts at will or will ourselves not to. It is the same for you, so do not think we are there to eavesdrop on you. I would say that it is a matter of courtesy of the most profound when we do not use our ability to listen in on conversations or thoughts that have nothing to do with us. On the other hand, those that do will float to us for we are responsible for all of the thoughts or the energies that project towards or away from us.

JOURNAL

There is something remarkably helpful in having our own thoughts on record, things we may forget and wish to return to, reminding ourselves of how we felt at that point and later how we change. That was the remarkable thing in it for me. I could look back and see how I felt about life at 30 and later how I saw it at 40. This was a helpful device in getting to know myself better. It was also a pleasure to have someone to speak to, someone who listened quietly and allowed me to express my thoughts. What a wonder that is, and will be for all who engage in journal writing. There is a true friend, that journal who awaits that ink to paper each night. There is a true friend who does not ever disappoint or discourage or argue, it takes the words you commit to it and keeps them there safely for eternity. That is what mine did at least and so they remain today. I am moved to think that my life and my thoughts are deemed so worthwhile that they are there on record and read by so many. This is the greatest to me that any man can achieve, for others to consider that his words are worthwhile, but I did not live my life thinking I was gifted or remarkable.

TIMELESS AND AGELESS

We are all timeless and ageless and yet we think so little of ourselves as humans. If we are born in the low circumstances, or what is deemed low because of a lack of income or proper clothes or housing, we find that we are less the men than we should be. If we are born to high circumstance, to society and material things, then we are more. In fact, it is often the lowest born of us who learn the greatest lessons of life and it is the highest born who learn few. We must recognize that the experiences we have in life are not to teach us how to become better property owners, they are to teach us that there is more than what lies before us there in the physical. How much more wise do you know the man to be who has lived close to the earth and survived than he who lives so high from it and surrounds himself in material things but they are mere dust at his fingertips and he is a shell of a man. It is not true that the best of us ascend for the best of us often descend and know little and less. All things must grow or they die. These are truths to be explored and understood and known..

DEFINING FORCE

Truth is the defining force of all things. It is not meant to deter or detract. It is not meant to defy or to stranglehold anyone. It is simply what is. Truth is boundless and yet solid and always the same. Hate and love are much the same. Truth is with the captor and the captive, with the slave and the freeman. There is wisdom and truth in all.

You do not defy truth. It simply exists and can be perceived and known simply. There is no devastating loss involved in truth. There is only loss in the miring down in that which it is not. For you see the less truth there is, the heavier and the more difficult things become. In the defiance of truth the body suffers, the mind suffers, and the truth that should lead is set aside. The soul suffers most though many do not see the decay.

FLYING

Flying is like a carnival ride - so distant and true and high and when it comes down we land back on earth and look around and we feel at rest but not at peace. What have we gained going up so high, only to land back down? The memory, the experience, and then we can transmit that energy to the thought that creates a higher place for us to stand. It isn't that we do not grow spontaneously. It is that we grow through wisdom and experience and reaching out into the bands of reality, learning and growing as we do. Drag yourself down every moment on things that do not matter and you will see that soon the unhappiness prevails, but build yourself up and live true to yourself and your ability to know and you will see the winds come and lift you to heights not before known.

HAPPINESS

Happiness is a fundamental law for when in true harmony happiness flows. Ignorance is not bliss for it will ultimately cause more decay than assent. Focus on your longing, your desire to reach and know more, and work to maintain your balance as you learn and grow even when confronted by the demons that are alive and want only to feed on the lost.

SUICIDE

Suicide is an impossibility. There is no getting away from ourselves. You cannot die, as much as you might want to die, you can simply change your circumstance and your company. Things are not so much different here than there. Think again, change your vision, look to the heavens for guidance and know that there is purpose in all things and eventually the truth will be known.

EARTH AND HEAVENS

I am torn between my ties to the earth and my ties to the heavens. I would, if I could, reach out and pull to me that element of earth that anchored me there and make it brighter by the taking, but I cannot lift to my nose the earth and smell it in the way I could do then, or listen to the silent night, knowing it is not so silent, for under every rock and behind every weed of the earth life exists and it is there for all to uncover. That is the magic of earth for it is teaming with life that does not end.

TECHNOLOGY AS WEAPONRY

The new weaponry - that is what I call it. Technology is weaponry that scars those who hold its weight in their hands.

DECEMBER 21, 2012

In time more energy will come to this planet and much will change, but it is not so that on that particular date there will be a sudden enlargement of consciousness or that the world will blink with a new eye and see further than ever before. Such change will eventually occur, if we continue to reach into the heavens and beyond, and it will be in ways we never anticipated. This new awakening will include the awareness of life on other planets.

PREPARING FOR THE FUTURE

There is a need to prepare for what is to come over the mountain. It is a time for taking into account all that you value in a true sense and at a deep level. Look around you for the love that is the sustaining force. We are so often rocked by changes that take place around us, but when we are connected to our true foundation then there is little that will rock us. When our intention is to gain knowledge, when we cultivate relationships that are based on love and true connection, when we desire to surpass the knowledge and wisdom and strength of past generations and then pass our knowledge on to the next, rather than allowing ourselves to devolve into the lowest and most base expressions of ourselves, then we will be in a better place. There is little that can be gained by acquiring material goods because you do not carry those goods with you. What you carry is the strength of your character, the depth of your wisdom and the fullness of your heart.

The truth is in the spirit. The truest concerns are spirit. You must understand that what we are as physical beings will pass, but the spirit does not. This truth, once fully known and understood, will change the world.

> *"The rule is to carry as little as possible."*
> *- Henry David Thoreau, Journal, 22 July 1857*

THE CHATTER

As to the chatter that has filled this manuscript, I happen to know that there is a farm nearby where such chatter is always the main course at dinner. How funny is that? If we chatter on enough then we are preoccupied and do not hesitate or stop and listen and see what is on our plates. What is on your plate today?

The world spins on in such a motion and calibrated it would defy all of man's minds to determine what could push with such force, what could create with such force, what could make this world to be.

207

Chapter Twenty-seven
Bathing in the Light of the Universe

"We are in essence the God to which we seek."

*"The most glorious fact in my experience is not anything that I have
done or may hope to do, but a transient thought, or vision, or dream,
which I have had. I would give all the wealth of the world, and all the
deeds of all the heroes, for one true vision. But how can I communicate
with the gods, who am a pencil-maker on the earth, and not be insane?"*
- Henry David Thoreau,
A Week on the Concord and Merrimack Rivers (1849)

That was the question I asked myself throughout this
process, well not the pencil-maker part, but there were very few
people in my life during the time I was having this experience and
writing this book who I could talk to about it honestly without them
thinking that I had in fact lost my mind. Even when I revealed my
experience to those I knew in the UFO community, who were used to
stretching the limits of belief, I found myself confronting doubters.
It seems the existence of alien beings is more believable than that of
disembodied spirits, because aliens are presumed to be a part of the
physical realm, but are they? That may be a topic for consideration
at another time.

There seems to be a limitation for many when it comes to
understanding anything that falls outside of their own well
established and firmly held view of reality. This is nothing new to
me. It is something I have experienced all my life. Never really
talking about what I am seeing or doing is a technique I developed as

209

a child rather than having my reality dismissed as fantasy by my mother, who was quite good at doing that, or being teased relentlessly by my older siblings. I learned early on that many were unaware that there was another realm that existed beyond the physical world and in most cases it would be better for me not to mention it at all.

In this quote from his March 5, 1853 journal entry Thoreau describes his feelings after an encounter he had with some scientifically minded disbelievers.

> *"I felt that it would be to make myself the laughing-stock of the scientific community to describe to them that branch of science which specially interests me, in as much as they do not believe in a science which deals with the higher law. So I was obliged to speak to their condition and describe to them that poor part of me which alone they can understand. The fact is I am a mystic, a transcendentalist, and a natural philosopher to boot. Now I think of it, I should have told them at once that I was a transcendentalist. That would have been the shortest way of telling them that they would not understand my explanation."*

In the following transmissions Thoreau addresses the limitations that exist for those who do not believe in a non-physical reality.

FANTASY

There is nothing that can be revealed to anyone who has not yet reached this place within. That I believe is true. If you cannot reach within you and find that truest you, then you cannot understand the message of those of us who do. You may see us as fools who indulge in fantasy, while you indulge in reality, but my fantasy is more real than your scientific reality will ever be.

LIGHT

There are many who see only that the substance of an individual ends with the death of the body and that without physical form there can be no strength and solidity to the being but that is untrue. We remain as full and vital as before, if not more so, for we have bathed in the waters of the truths of the universe and we are buoyed by the knowledge that fills us. We resonate in full energy with a vibration and glow. The light of the other side is what fuels us. We are not puffs of smoke that blow in and out. We are solid and vital and alive, so alive, and we are aware of all things that have passed since our time.

PAST LIVES

We are each a repository for all of the lives we have lived. As a writer writes books and stories with many characters and circumstances and those books become the totality of that author's work, so the many lives we live become the totality of our soul's mission. We are each on our own individual journey that will eventually lead us back to the source. We are in essence the God to which we seek. That is the strangest and yet the most beautiful of all of the truths for it tells us that who we are is ever changing, and yet who we are at any given moment will always be.

We are consciousness in pure form, transferring only a part of our awareness into the physical with each life we live. The thoughts, ideas and visions of man are first born here on this side and there is reciprocity, a mirroring that is involved when influences take place.

ON DYING

At the time that I passed I found myself adrift in the clouds and then I saw light, bright and brilliant light, and the clouds parted to allow for that light and I felt myself moved into it. There I found those who I had known and loved and who had passed before me. Dearest Wallie was there with his hand out to greet me, and then my father and my brother, all in their hardiest expressions and ready to embrace and welcome me and to forgive all that needed to be forgiven for ways in which I had or had not been toward them, as I also offered forgiveness to them. There was then a recognition and a revelation as others appeared who I had known and admired or loved and who had passed but were here, so solid and alive. What a miracle that was. How wonderful to see that in God's heaven there could be this brilliancy of light and power and that those who I had loved and shed so many tears over were well and happy and fit and had been watching. They knew all I had done, all I was meant to do, and all I would yet be able to do there.

When the greetings were over, when I found that my grandmother's arms and my uncle's humor had fed me enough then I turned to the viewing of what passed back on earth and I understood that the events that were taking place there bore for me some responsibility. That is I felt they did, and I could see that I could reach up into the strength of heaven and draw down the wisdom that I needed and could then pass it along. I could be the conduit who brings wisdom to those who I loved and remained there or to those in power who needed and sought guidance through the words I had written. I could bring wisdom to them through spirit and that is what I did.

MEMORIES OF THE PAST

Memories of the past are keeping me tied there. It is difficult for me to rise above the impressions of a life when the aftermath of that life is so strong. Everyone who reads my words and who comes to that place where I lived in their attempt to connect to me or to the peace they believe I experienced there is helping to keep me tied there. In some ways we are all held back by the intensity of this focus on one particular time, place and man.

EXPECTATIONS

The world did not live up to the measure of the expectations that I had of it, neither were the people who I wanted them to be. That was my flaw - to expect pure transformation, to expect revelation from all men and women. Could they not see what I could see? No, they could not. They were there to live and learn at their own pace. The most worthwhile relationship that I had in my life was not with anyone in particular, it was with the divine nature of all things.

ANOTHER PATH

There are many who would choose another path for themselves if they could recognize that they have the power to do so. They would strike out on their own and make the lives that they wanted. It is through the act of doing that we learn, not through the act of not doing it. It is the nature of man to know there is more and to long for it.

* * *

Chapter Twenty-eight
An Altered State of Consciousness; The Contact Passage

"I fear not spirits, ghosts of which I am one."

In the following transmission Thoreau is referring to a moment that occurred during a trip I made to Mt. Katahdin in Northern Maine in May 2008, when I stood on a hillside outside of Millinocket, Maine and looked out upon the "great mountain" for the first time.

> I want you to see now in the distance that glorious image of the mountain that you once beheld with your weakened eyes and asked what is it that draws me here now and what is it that drew him then? What called to me when I climbed it and saw it for the first time was then and is now, spirit.

I learned about Mt. Katahdin through Connie Baxter Marlow's book, *The Great Mountain*, and her film series, *The American Evolution*, that featured Thoreau scholar, Bradley P. Dean, Ph.D. In the film Brad discusses the significance of a passage from Thoreau's book, *The Maine Woods (1864)*, in which Thoreau describes a moment of heightened awareness that he experienced while climbing Mt. Katahdin in September 1846. What Thoreau wrote has become known as the "Contact! Passage," a portion of which is as follows:

*"I stand in awe of my body. This matter to which I am bound has
become so strange to me. I fear not spirits, ghosts of which I am one.
That my body might, but I fear bodies. I tremble to meet them. What is
this Titan that has possession of me? Talk of mysteries, think of our life
in nature, daily to be shown matter, to come in contact with it, rock,
trees, the wind on our cheeks, the solid earth, the actual world, the
common sense. Contact, contact... Who are we? Where are we?"*
- Henry David Thoreau, The Maine Woods (1864)

For those who are familiar with the term "out of body" experience" or who have experienced similar events themselves, it is easy to recognize this moment of revelation for Thoreau as just that. The term "out of body experience" was first coined by Charles T. Tart, Ph.D., a man who was internationally known for his work in the field of human consciousness. Tart wrote the following description of an OOBE in his introduction to the book, *Journeys Out of the Body,*" by Robert A. Monroe, founder of the Monroe Institute in Faber, Virginia, a cutting edge research institute in the field of human consciousness:

"The experience of an OOBE is usually one of the most profound experiences of a person's life, and radically alters his beliefs. This is usually expressed as, "I no longer *believe* in survival of death or an immortal soul, I *know* that I will survive death." The person feels that he has directly experienced being alive and conscious without his physical body, and therefore knows that he possesses some kind of soul that will survive bodily death."[36]

Thoreau's description of his experience atop Mr. Katahdin in September 1846 supports this statement. He uses the word, "contact" to describe the moment when his awareness shifts and he comes into full contact with spirit for the first time. In this state of disassociation from his body, he looks upon it in awe and can no longer recognize himself as that vessel. At that point, Thoreau states that he no longer fears spirits or ghosts because while perceiving things from that vantage point, somewhere outside of his body, he recognizes that he is indeed one of them. He is spirit and now he

---

[36] From introduction to "Journeys Out of the Body" by Robert A. Monroe, published by Doubleday and Company in 1971.

fears the very body from which he has sprung. He looks around at the matter that surrounds him and recognizes it as just that, dull matter, while at the same time he is experiencing the grandness of spirit.

Brad's analysis of Thoreau's contact passage was extensive. He wrote and spoke about it many times during the years and months leading up to his death. His observations were not limited by any conventional scientific or academic view because he believed in the reality of spirit and found confirmation of it in Thoreau's description of this moment atop Mt. Katahdin. In a scene from the *American Evolution* that was filmed outside at the library in Concord, MA in 2002, Brad talks about the inability of most Thoreauvians to comprehend the significance of the passage. He states that most dismiss it as a moment when Thoreau is overwhelmed and linguistically challenged, unable to find the words to describe the beauty he sees around him.

I was at First Parish Church in Concord in July 2012, ten years after Brad had made this statement at the library, when the keynote speaker for the Thoreau Society's annual gathering expressed almost exactly what Brad had described as the typical Thoreauvian's analysis of the contact passage. This is a colossal misunderstanding of a key moment in Thoreau's work and although it was amusing to hear it articulated almost exactly as Brad had said it would be, it was also sad to hear this scholar who so much fuss was being made over by the usual academics at the gathering that year and since get it so wrong.

In addition to the *American Evolution* film series, Brad also wrote about the contact passage in the Scholar's Notes that he wrote for the *Life With Principle: Thoreau's Voice in Our Time* DVD-ROM program produced by the Thoreau Society, shortly before he himself passed into spirit. To me, the fact that he wrote the following words so soon before his own passing only makes them more poignant.

In those Scholar's Notes Brad states:

"...commentators suggest that Thoreau leaves unanswered the two questions at the end of the passage: *"Who are we? Where are we?"* But again, he in fact answers both of those questions in the passage when he says, *"I fear not spirits, ghosts, of which I am one, -* that *my body might..."* Clearly, *who* we are is "spirits, ghosts." And *where* are each of us? Each of us as a spirit is inside a body. In short, we are embodied spirits."

and he goes on to say:

In other words, we think and believe and behave as if we are bodies. Because we think and believe and behave this way, life appears to be *mean* to us. But if we put aside that *appearance* of who we are – of ourselves as nothing but bodies – and realize that what we *really* are is spirits, then life would be sublime,..[..]."

The revelation of the contact passage is that we still exist, full and intact, even when outside of our physical bodies. Once that distinction is experienced and understood, clarity is attained and a resultant joy ensues. The simple meanness of life is lifted as the revelation of the grandness of all things is revealed. Contact is made, contact with the boundless energy and possibility of the spirit. All that is living will keep on living! It is only the material, the dull matter of the earth plane that will cease.

Brad also wrote an essay that was entitled, *Natural History, Romanticism and Thoreau,* and was published posthumously in 2007 in *American Wilderness: A New History* edited by Michael Lewis. In it, Brad references what he calls "the eternal return". It is a reference to the way that nature recycles its physical matter. The physical body will continue to die and be recycled through nature, but the spirit will withstand all of nature's assaults on the physical, and will continue to live when the physical body is gone.

There on Mt. Katahdin, Thoreau saw the mystery of life in nature, as we are confronted daily with elements of the material world such as, *"the rocks, the trees, the wind on our cheeks, the actual world, the common sense."* He saw that these things that are physically experienced and understood to exist are more transient than the substance that lies within them, and he saw himself both as the body that makes contact with the physical world, and as the spirit who occupies that body. *"Who are we? Where are we?"* We are spirit manifesting, for a time at least, in a physical body in a material world.

In his moment of revelation atop Mt. Katahdin, the distinction between the physical and the spiritual aspects of life became even clearer to Thoreau, and he believed that in that moment contact with spirit had been made.

In *Walden*, published in 1854, nearly eight years after this incident, Thoreau states:

> "Not till we are lost, in other words not till we have lost the world, do we begin to find ourselves, and realize where we are and the infinite extent of our relations."

Anyone with a basic intelligence can inventory and catalog the elements that make up the physical world, but it takes a certain awareness, an intuitive intelligence, to understand that part of the universe that cannot be easily related to through the physical senses. Thoreau was a master at this. In his journal dated April 3, 1842, he writes:

> "On one side of man is the actual, and on the other the ideal. The former is the province of the reason; it is even a divine light when directed upon it, but it cannot reach forward into the ideal without blindness. The moon was made to rule all night but the sun to rule by day. Reason will be but a pale cloud like the moon when one ray of divine light comes to illumine the soul."

And in a journal entry dated July 2, 1857, he states:

"Many an object is not seen, though it falls within the range of our visual ray, because it does not come within the range of our intellectual ray, i.e. we are not looking for it. So, in the largest sense, we find only the world we look for."

In his essay, *Life Without Principle (1863)* Thoreau states:

"Knowledge does not come to us by details, but in flashes of light from heaven".

So, what value do we take from Thoreau's work if we read his words, consider his thoughts, but never allow ourselves to follow the path that they lay out for us? Unlike those who are merely scholars of a subject and not themselves experiencers, I speak as one who has experienced spirit in a real way, I speak with a deep conviction and I speak from the heart when I say that any valid understanding of Thoreau's work must recognize his fundamental belief in a consciousness that exists outside of the physical form.

Thoreau believes it is by connecting to the divine within us that the greatest fulfillment and happiness in life can be found. But once found, how does this knowledge change our lives? How do we proceed differently? Does the understanding that there is a divine source that fuels all of us change the way we treat each other? Thoreau believed that once connected to the spiritual dimension, the individual would act in adherence to the higher laws but he also felt that the capacity for such divinely inspired living was rare. In *Walden* he states:

"The millions are awake enough for physical labor; but only one in a million is awake enough for effective intellectual exertion, only one in a hundred million to a poetic or divine life. To be awake is to be alive."

I look forward to the day when our understanding of consciousness and of ourselves as spiritual not physical beings has advanced to the point that when someone reports that they have made a connection with someone who has passed on that we don't dismiss them as a kook, but instead understand what Thoreau himself understood that we do survive the death of the body, and for those who have the ability it is possible to connect in substantial ways to those who live on in spirit.

Thoreau stood out from the crowd in Concord, not simply because he didn't wear the correct clothes or didn't like to engage in the habits of common people, but because of his awareness of spirit. He stood out because an awakened individual cannot reside in lock step with those who are not awake. He simply could not conform to their conformity and therefore, sought out his own path, his own way and he found it.

To fully understand Thoreau and his views we must awaken ourselves to the reality of spirit. With that, I conclude this book in part where I started it, with the statement that I put on my website in 2009. Like everything else I was writing back then I feel it was deeply inspired but I consider these words to be my own and not Thoreau's. They emphasize the enduring spirit of all of us and I believe they set the pace for the transmissions that followed.

"I believe that if you pause for five minutes each day, close your eyes and allow yourself to look within, you will find your truest self and it is in that recognition that you will find your greatest joy.

Open your hearts and minds to the possibilities because that spirit within you is the you that will never end. Your life is yesterday, today and every tomorrow. All who ever were still are and always will be."

* * *

Chapter Twenty-nine
In the Still Quiet

I began to sense the rhythm and cadence of his speech...

At the law firm in Boston where I worked the evening shift it was common that I would find myself alone there in the later evening hours, after the attorneys had gone home and after the evening's work had been done. It was a period of still quiet when I could look out the window and enjoy the lights of the city, or I could spend some time reading or researching online. It was also a time when I could often close my eyes and, during the years when the channeling was the strongest, I could easily connect to spirit.

One night, as I sat quietly at my desk reading Thoreau's essay, *Life Without Principle*[37] online I found myself connecting with Thoreau again. This time, as I read his words on the computer screen, I began to sense the rhythm and cadence of his speech in a way I had never done before. Thoreau was reading to me, or I might better say he was reading along with me, the essay he had written over 150 years before. That was a surprising moment to say the least and a deeply moving one that helped me to release any remaining doubts I had about this experience that had so greatly impacted my life. That was the moment when I fully accepted that it was in fact the spirit of Henry David Thoreau who I had been communicating with all along. How extraordinary this experience was for me. What a miracle! What a gift!

---

[37] *Life Without Principle* was first a lecture entitled *What Shall It Profit?* that Thoreau delivered in Providence, RI in December 1854. He edited it for publication before he passed, and it was published as *Life Without Principle* in The Atlantic Monthly in October 1863.

Acknowledgements

There are many individuals in the spiritual community in the greater Boston, Massachusetts area to whom I am most grateful for the guidance and much needed confirmation they provided to me throughout this most extraordinary experience. The most significant of course being the Reverend Barbara Szafranski at Angelica of the Angels in Salem, Massachusetts, who with such ease made that initial contact with Henry Thoreau and Brad Dean and shared the message that would change my life. My gratitude also to her partner, now in spirit, George Fraggos, who was there early on encouraging me to follow the intuition that had brought me to Concord, Massachusetts in the first place. I thank the others as well who were there as supportive voices throughout this experience and provided much needed confirmation to me, often over the smallest things, when I most needed it and that meant so much.

Cathryn McIntyre
February 2018